MAMMA, SI MANGIA?

(Mama, Are We Eating?)

A Florentine Son Shares
His Feisty Mother's Recipes

BY GIAMPAOLO FALLAI WITH LORAINE PAGE
ILLUSTRATIONS BY ANNA JURINICH

bright sky press

bright sky press

Albany, Texas
New York, New York

10   9   8   7   6   5   4   3   2   1

Library of Congress Cataloging-in-Publication Data

Fallai, Giampaolo, 1948-
    Mamma, si mangia? = Mamma, are we eating? : a Florentine son shares his feisty
mother's recipes / by Giampaolo Fallai with Loraine Page ; illustrated by Anna Jurinich.
        p. cm.
    In English.
    ISBN 1-931721-09-2 (alk. paper)
    1.Cookery, Italian. 2. Fallai, Mafalda. 3. Cooks—Italy—Florence--Biography. I. Title:
    Mamma, are we eating?. II. Page, Loraine, 1952- III. Title.

TX723 .F332 2002
641.5945--dc21

                                                                    2001052923

Book and cover design by Karen Ocker
Edited by Bob Somerville

Printed in the United States of America

To the person who influenced my life the most. It is because of her continued support and motherly critique that this book exists. This is for you, *Mamma*—90 years young, still a great cook, and the best mother anyone could wish for! *Con tanto amore, tuo figlio Giampaolo.*

Also, in loving memory of my friend, my fishing companion, my best supporter—my father, Renato. *Ciao babbo.* Wherever you are, I love you always.

Contents

Recipe List

SAVORIES

Coccoli (Fried Dough Balls), 94

Cozze Ripiene (Stuffed Mussels), 54

Foglie di Salvia Ripiene (Giant Sage Leaves Stuffed), 88

Olive Ripiene (Stuffed Olives), 17

Pinzimonio (Fennel with Olive Oil), 96

SOUPS AND SAUCES

Pasta & Fagioli (Pasta and Bean Soup), 15

Pummarola (Puréed Tomato Sauce), 111

Salsa Piccante (Pungent Sauce), 112

Sincero (Homemade Beef Bouillon), 110

Stracciatella (Egg Drop Soup Italian Style), 97

Sugo D'Aragosta alla Mafalda (Lobster Sauce Mafalda Style), 55

MEAT, CHICKEN & FISH

Arista (Roast Pork Loin), 119

Coda alla Vaccinara (Oxtail Vaccinara Style), 25

Involtini alla Cacciatora (Rolled-Up Veal Cutlets Hunter Style), 62

Involtini Prelibati (Succulent Wraps), 63

Pollo Fritto all' Anna (Anna's Famous Fried Chicken), 126

Scaloppine al Basilico (Scaloppini with Basil), 73

Scaloppine alla Livornese (Chops Livornese Style), 61

Tonno e Fagioli (Tuna and Cannellini Beans), 98

Vitello Tonnato (Veal with Tuna Sauce), 64

VEGETABLE DISHES

Cannelloni di Crespelle (Crepes Cannelloni), 82

Cavolo Ubriaco (Drunken Cauliflower), 53

Cipolle Gelatinate (Onions in Gelatin), 86

Fagioli all'Uccelletto (Beans Cooked Like Small Birds), 120

Insalata a tre Fagioli (Three-Bean Salad), 26

Involtini di Melanzane alla Mafalda (Eggplant Rollatini Mafalda Style), 74

Panzanella (Country Bread with Onions, Tomatoes, and Basil), 27

Radicchio Strascinato (Sautéed Radicchio), 25

Uova al Pomodoro (Eggs and Tomatoes), 29

Zucchini al Limone (Zucchini with Lemon Sauce), 57

Zucchini Ripiene (Stuffed Zucchini Squash), 56

RICE, PASTA & PIZZA

Gnocchi alla Romana (Dumplings Roman Style), 16

Lasagne alla Mafalda (Lasagne Mafalda Style), 81

Pizza al Formaggio per Pasqua (Easter Cheese Pizza), 18

Pizza Margherita (Pizza with Artichokes, Mushrooms and Ham), 112

Ravioli Ignudi (Naked Ravioli), 84

Riso Millegusti (Thousand-Flavor Rice), 114

Spaghetti a Fiori di Basilico (Spaghetti with Basil Flowers), 73

Spaghetti Aglio e Olio (Spaghetti with Garlic and Oil), 95

Spaghetti al Tartufo (Spaghetti with Truffle Sauce), 89

DESSERTS

Cenci (Fried Pastry Dough), 109

Crema Caramellata (Crème Caramel), 39

Jam Crostata (Criss-Cross Cake), 37

Paste con Crema Chantilly (Cream Puffs with Chantilly Cream), 35

Schiacciata con L'uva (Grape Cake), 71

Torta di Zucca Gialla alla Fiorentina (Pumpkin Pie Florentine Style), 40

Zuppa Inglese (English Cake), 36

Acknowledgments

$\mathcal{F}$irst, thanks go to friend and neighbor Loraine Page. Her skill as a writer enabled her to take the germ of an idea and transform it into a completed book. Thank you for your enthusiasm, Loraine! Thanks also go to my wife, Anna Jurinich, for her devotion to this project, especially in the form of all the drawings and the beautiful front cover art she provided. I'm grateful to you, Loraine and Anna, for helping me honor my mother in this way.

Friends and family members graciously agreed to test recipes for us. Their time, effort, and expense are all greatly appreciated. Thanks go to the following expert cooks: Maria Caprara, Sue Gillen, Merly Grdovich, Sheryl Heller, Suzanne Jack, Mira Jurinich, Ann Marie Malvagna, Joan Miller, Anna Morris, Sylvia Rabinowitz, and Anna Stanghellini.

Thank you, Kate Hartson of Bright Sky Press, for liking our book so much and for all the compliments you bestowed on my cooking.

Thanks to Bob Somerville for being a great editor and making this book the best it can be (and for trying out some of the recipes, too!).

Thanks also to Twin Peaks Geeks for keeping pivotal computers up and running throughout.

And thanks, of course, to Mafalda for her zest for life.

CHAPTER ONE

Mafalda, my mother...

My mother has been obsessed with food all her life. When she was only seven years old and living with her family in the town of Piediluco, in the region of Umbria, she used to scramble from one hilltop house to another in search of a tastier meal than the one her own mother was preparing.

Getting her own way and loving food with a passion—these traits, already evident in such a young girl, emerged even stronger when Mafalda became a grown woman. Not surprisingly, those who love my mother would agree on two things about her: She is headstrong and she is a great cook.

Mafalda later moved to Florence, in the region of Tuscany. It was here, in a second-floor terraced apartment, that she set up housekeeping with my father, Renato, in the years just before World War II. Some of the cooking she did for Renato reflected her Umbrian heritage, such as her **Pasta & Fagioli (Pasta and Bean Soup), Gnocchi alla Romana (Dumplings Roman Style),** and **Olive Ripiene (Stuffed Olives)**. Even a traditional Easter dish we had in my house when I was growing up has Umbrian roots—the **Pizza al Formaggio per Pasqua (Easter Cheese Pizza)**.

I always thought my mother should have opened her own restaurant, because her dishes would have been very popular. And indeed she wanted to. But my father was a shoemaker and a traditional sort of man. He liked to have my mother cooking in his own kitchen—for obvious reasons, as you'll find out for yourself as soon as you try one of her recipes.

Pasta & Fagioli

(Pasta and Bean Soup)

To this day, I can't find another version of this bean soup that I like better than my mother's. Whenever I go into a restaurant that serves pasta & fagioli, I try it, but I'm always disappointed. In this recipe, pay attention to how my mother has a special way of making sure some of the beans stay whole instead of all getting smashed or puréed.

INGREDIENTS

½ lb. ditalini (also known as "little thimbles" because of their shape; you can substitute any small pasta that is hollow inside)

1 lb. dried white kidney beans

5-6 thick slices imported prosciutto, coarsely chopped

1 large red onion, chopped

3-4 cloves garlic, peeled

1 16-oz. can tomatoes

2 chicken or beef bouillon cubes

1 sprig fresh rosemary, or 1 tsp. dried

4 sage leaves

¼ cup olive oil

4 cups water

salt and pepper to taste

PREPARATION

- Soak the beans in water for 24 hours or at least overnight, making sure the water is just above the top of the beans. Check periodically and add more water as necessary.

- In the same pot, cook the beans over medium-low heat for about 1 to 1 ½ hours; keep stirring so they don't stick to the bottom, and add more water if it starts getting low. Taste one or two beans from time to time to make sure they aren't overcooking.

- Divide the beans in three parts and set aside.

- In a large pot, heat the olive oil over medium heat. Add the onions and prosciutto. Sauté for a few minutes until the onion is golden brown. Add the tomatoes and cook for 10 to 15 minutes. Add two parts of the beans; put the rest aside to be used later. Add the water, garlic, bouillon cubes, rosemary, sage leaves, and salt and pepper. Cook over medium heat for 10 more minutes.

- Let cool, then purée all of the above in a food processor. Pour it back into the pot. Add the pasta and let cook until tender, approximately 10 to 15 minutes. If the soup is too thick, add water. When done, add the remaining beans, stir gently, and serve hot.

- Serves 4 to 6.

Gnocchi alla Romana

(Dumplings Roman Style)

In Umbria, where my mother was born, this is a common dish. I use it as a main course because it's very filling. Our two sons love it— we all do, especially when the gnocchi are cooked enough so that the cheese gets a little dark on the outside.

INGREDIENTS

¾ cup semolina (a yellow grain found in the flour section of the supermarket) or farina (found in the cereal section)

3 cups milk

1 tsp. salt

pinch of nutmeg

2 eggs

2 cups grated parmigiano cheese

8 Tbsp. butter (1 stick)

pepper to taste

PREPARATION

• Cook the semolina or farina according to the cooking instructions on the box; set aside to cool. When cooled to a lukewarm temperature, add the milk, salt, nutmeg, eggs, 1 cup of the cheese, 4 Tbsp. of the butter, and pepper. Mix well and spread the batter evenly, about ½ inch thick, on a wooden board previously covered with wax paper. Place in the refrigerator, on the board, for 1 hour.

• Once cooled, take out and use a drinking glass about 2 ½ inches in diameter to cut as many circles as you can. With the strips left over from the circle cutting, reshape again into ½-inch-thick batter; cut into circles again, and repeat until all the batter is used up.

• On an ovenproof plate, arrange the circles, one next to the other and somewhat overlapping. Dribble some of the butter on top and sprinkle with ½ cup of parmigiano cheese. Place in a 350° F. preheated oven; cook until the top gets light to medium brown, about 1 ½ hours.

• Serve hot or cold with parmigiano cheese sprinkled on top.

• Serves 4 to 6.

Olive Ripiene

(Stuffed Olives)

Make this for your next party. When I put it out on a platter at get-togethers in my home, invariably someone will say that they never would have thought of stuffing something so small as an olive. And it's true that this dish is a bit time consuming to prepare. But oh, is it good, and it presents beautifully!

NOTE: *This dish has to be refrigerated for 12 hours or more, so you will have to make it the day before you plan to serve it.*

INGREDIENTS

1 lb. Spanish or Greek green (or black if you can't find green) pitted olives

10 slices mortadella, finely cubed

1 ¹/₂ cups grated romano cheese

¹/₂ tsp. freshly grated nutmeg

1 ¹/₂ cups Italian-style breadcrumbs

¹/₂ cup extra virgin olive oil

1 ¹/₂ cups flour

1 egg, beaten

oil for frying

PREPARATION

- Mix the mortadella, cheese, half of the breadcrumbs, oil, and nutmeg. Mix well to make a paste.

- Fill the olives one by one and then dip them in flour (put the flour in a plastic bag, add the olives, and shake gently). Once the olives are floured, dip them one by one into the beaten egg, then into the breadcrumbs. Set aside for a day. (Do not stack them one on top of the other.)

- The next day, heat the oil to a medium temperature. Put the olives a few at a time into the oil. Turn them a few times until golden brown.

- Serve hot as an appetizer or as a side dish.

- Serves 4 to 6.

HOW TO KEEP HOT DISHES HOT

For food that has to be served very hot, put the plates you're going to use in a large pot filled with hot water. Carefully, wearing rubber gloves, take the plates out one by one as you're ready to serve. Give them a quick swipe with a dishtowel and get the hot food on them before they cool.

Pizza al Formaggio per Pasqua

(Easter Cheese Pizza)

My mother made this every Easter. It was part of our holiday ritual: Hard-boil the eggs, make the Easter Cheese Pizza, and then get the house ready for the priest who would come to bless our rooms and everyone who lived in them—human and animal! We would anticipate the arrival of cousins, uncles, and aunts. My mother would anticipate the compliments on her cooking. But before diving into the food, we took it to Holy Easter Mass to have it blessed. Then the celebrations could begin.

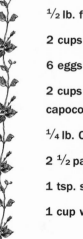

INGREDIENTS

4 cups flour

$1/2$ lb. fresh pecorino cheese, grated

2 cups grated parmigiano cheese

6 eggs

2 cups cubed capocollo or prosciutto

$1/4$ lb. Crisco-type shortening

2 $1/2$ packets active dry yeast

1 tsp. salt

1 cup water, more if necessary

PREPARATION

- Prepare the yeast like this: In a small bowl, place the yeast in ½ cup lukewarm water and mix until the yeast is diluted well; add 2 Tbsp. of the flour and stir well. Set aside covered, in a warm location, until the yeast starts bubbling and doubling in size—about 10 minutes.

- Mix this with the rest of the flour, water, eggs, cheeses, capocollo or prosciutto, shortening, and salt.

- Start kneading all the ingredients together, just like making bread.

Work it well for at least 30 to 45 minutes. Divide the dough in half, place in 2 high-rimmed round

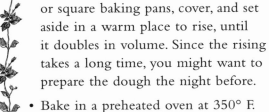

or square baking pans, cover, and set aside in a warm place to rise, until it doubles in volume. Since the rising takes a long time, you might want to prepare the dough the night before.

- Bake in a preheated oven at 350° F. until golden brown.

- Serve at room temperature.

- Serves 6 to 8.

(Hint: This pizza lasts a long time if kept refrigerated in a plastic bag.)

FRESH BREATH

In Italy, we don't worry too much about garlic breath. If it bothers you, chew on some fresh parsley or fennel.

Perseus proudly holding the crown of
Florentine cuisine: Zucchini Flowers . . .

CHAPTER TWO

A boy learns about food...

Even when I was only a young boy, it was apparent to my mother and me that I shared her love of food. I watched mesmerized as she diced, chopped, sauteéd, simmered, stirred, canned, and baked. My sister didn't have much interest and for many years wouldn't do much more than boil water.

My mother took advantage of my interest in cooking by sending me out for ingredients when she needed them. I still hold to the philosophy she taught me then: If you're going to cook something, make sure you get all the ingredients. Otherwise, don't even bother.

Sometimes I would be sent to the market, but other times my mother wanted me to go out and pick something from the fields. It could be berries for making jam or dandelion leaves for **Radicchio Strascinato (Sautéed Radicchio).** She sent me out for whatever she didn't have growing in pots on the terrace or couldn't get from friends who had gardens.

I remember one time I came home from school to find my mother frantic. She had eaten a dish prepared by a friend, Attilia, and it was quite special.

"This was the most delicious dish I've had in years," said my mother. "But that stubborn woman would not divulge the recipe! Every bite I took gave me more pieces of the puzzle, though, and now I am sure I have it. I have shopped for all the ingredients except one—and that is where you come in, Giampaolo."

The dish was called **Coda alla Vaccinara (Oxtail Vaccinara Style)** and it needed juniper berries, which could be picked on a hillside about ten miles away. I did as my mother asked and many hours later, tired and sweaty, handed her a small bag of what I very much hoped were juniper berries (they were).

On most days my mother would ask me what I wanted for supper. "Anything you feel like making, Ma," was my usual response, because I knew that anything she prepared would be delicious. But once in a while I'd say, "Gee, it's been a long time since you made such and such"—and faster than you could blink she'd write a list of ingredients and send me on my way.

In the summer I'd request cold dishes like **Insalata a tre Fagioli (Three-Bean Salad)**, which required me to pick fresh sage, or **Panzanella (Country Bread with Onions, Tomatoes,**

and Basil), a delicious dish with stale bread as one of its ingredients. Sometimes, when the red, juicy tomatoes were ripening on the vines and the intoxicating smell of basil was in the air, I'd ask my mother to make ***Uova al Pomodoro (Eggs and Tomatoes)***. Out I'd be sent to a nearby farm to pick the tomatoes and basil, and even to remove freshly laid eggs from under the hens.

In the spring when I was sent to the banks of a nearby stream to pick wild herbs for either food or medicinal purposes—my mother was well versed in the health properties of many plants, having worked at an apothecary before she was married—I'd sometimes stop to pick a bouquet of wild violets for my mother. I remember those scented violets with nostalgia because never again have I found any that smell so sweet.

Lest you think everything was roses all the time between my mother and me, I should tell you that I misbehaved at times. And when I did, my mother never hesitated to grab a wooden spoon off the kitchen wall and come after me. Usually, I grabbed the spoon from her hand and tossed it off the balcony. To this day, wooden spoons can still be seen on the red-tiled roof of the building next door!

I think my mother is the most wonderful woman in the world (except for my wife, Anna, of course). She is a strong woman, full of zest for life, and she can be, well, domineering at times. Whenever I tell her she is too much, she says, "Remember, you only have one mother." To which I always reply, "*Meno male*," which means, somewhat sarcastically, "Oh, lucky me."

Radicchio Strascinato

(Sautéed Radicchio)

In Florence, the arrival of spring would find everyone suffering from cabin fever, but no one was affected as much as my mother. As soon as the temperature climbed a few degrees, she would shoo me outside to search for the elusive radicchio selvatico. After a few hours, I was usually able to present her with a meager picking of pale green leaves—so tender I had to be careful not to damage them. You won't have any trouble finding radicchio, though: They're the very young, early-springtime leaves of the familiar dandelion. This radicchio is not to be mistaken for the longer, cultivated greens found in upscale supermarkets. These dandelion greens are smaller. As a safety measure, only pick where you know the dandelions have not been sprayed with pesticides, herbicides, or any other contaminants. The ones that grow in your own yard might be safest. You can also find farm-raised young dandelion greens in a very good produce store, and even in the supermarket.

INGREDIENTS

1 lb. radicchio, boiled for 10 minutes (do not overcook) and coarsely chopped

2-3 cloves garlic, chopped

4-5 Tbsp. extra virgin olive oil

salt and pepper to taste

PREPARATION

- In a heavy skillet, sauté the garlic in the olive oil at medium heat until the garlic is golden brown (make sure you don't burn it). When the garlic is ready, add the radicchio, and toss it around for two or three minutes. Add salt and pepper. Serve hot. Makes a great side dish.

- Serves 4.

Coda alla Vaccinara

(Oxtail Vaccinara Style)

When my mother was making this "secret" recipe, she was like a forensic scientist at work. But when all her tedious measuring and tasting was done—let me tell you, it was worth the effort!

INGREDIENTS

2 lbs. oxtail pieces (you can substitute veal or pork chops)

$1/4$ cup flour

1 large red onion, thinly sliced

$1/4$ cup extra virgin olive oil

2 cups dry red wine

1 16-oz. can chopped tomatoes

1 cup beef or chicken broth

10 juniper berries

5 allspice berries, or 1 tsp. powdered allspice

salt and pepper to taste

PREPARATION

- Wash the pieces of oxtail or chops, then place in a plastic bag with flour. Shake well, making sure all the pieces are well floured. Take out and set aside.

- For the next steps, I prefer a pressure cooker because it's easier, the flavor is more intense, and the meat comes out more tender. But you can use a conventional pot with a cover. Set your burner to medium high, and place the sliced onion in the pressure cooker or pot with the olive oil. When the oil starts getting hot, add the oxtail or chops and quickly brown them all over. Then add the wine and cook until most of it evaporates.

- Set the burner to medium low, and add the allspice, broth, tomatoes, juniper berries, salt, and freshly ground pepper to taste.

- Continue cooking for approximately two hours, making sure the meat doesn't stick to the bottom of the pan. If using a pressure cooker, make sure to cover right away and put the heat up to medium. When the pot whistles and steam begins to escape, turn the heat to medium low and cook for only 20 minutes. Cool off

with the cover still on. After it cools, you can open it easily. Use the sauce over a good pasta, and serve the meat hot as a main dish.

- Serves 4.

Insalata a tre Fagioli

(Three-Bean Salad)

When the summer was too hot to even think of typical steamy Italian dishes, my mother would prepare cool, refreshing ones like this. It calls for fresh sage leaves, and you-know-who would be sent to get some.

INGREDIENTS

½ lb. dried cannellini beans

½ lb. dried pinto beans

½ lb. dried red kidney beans

2 cups water saved from boiled beans

1/2 cup extra virgin olive oil

10 fresh sage leaves, crushed between your fingers to release the flavor

1 onion, very thinly sliced

4 Tbsp. balsamic vinegar

salt and freshly ground pepper (this is a must) to taste

PREPARATION

NOTE: *The dried beans must be soaked for 24 hours. Wash them well, strain them, and place them in a large pot. Fill the pot with cold water, just enough to cover the beans. Keep checking throughout the 24 hours and add water if necessary to keep the beans just covered. After the soaking is finished, strain the beans, place them in the large pot, add cold water to cover the beans, and cook at low heat (stirring from time to time) for 1 1/2 to 2 hours. Keep checking the water to make sure it is still just above the beans. Don't overcook; test one or two beans for readiness— they should be soft to the bite but not too mushy. When done, drain (don't forget to save two cups of the water), and set aside.*

- In a large bowl, place the beans, saved water, crushed fresh sage leaves, sliced onion, and balsamic vinegar; mix gently. Add oil and salt, then mix again gently. Last but not least, sprinkle with freshly ground pepper and mix one more time.

- Cover and refrigerate for at least 2 hours.

PARTY PREPARATION

If the recipe allows, make the food a day before the party, or at least much earlier in the day, so you can enjoy the occasion, too!

- Serve cold.

- Can be served as a main dish, an accompaniment to a meat or poultry dish, or even as an appetizer.

- Serves 4 to 6.

Panzanella

(Country Bread with Onions, Tomatoes, and Basil)

Sometimes the temperature would reach 110° in Florence. On days like those, my father would come home from work in the evening and ask my mother if she would make a nice bowl of panzanella. It involves no cooking at all—just mix the ingredients and refrigerate. You might end up with onion breath after you eat this, but it's worth it!

INGREDIENTS

1 lb. stale Italian bread

1 large red onion, thinly sliced

6 Tbsp. extra virgin olive oil

2 cups water

8 Tbsp. (or to taste) red wine vinegar

2 cups whole fresh basil leaves

1 large ripe tomato, sliced

1 tsp. coarse kosher salt
(does not wilt the basil or tomato)
and pepper to taste

PREPARATION

- In a bowl, mix the water with
  4 Tbsp. of the vinegar. Tear the
  bread into large pieces and gently
  immerse in the water and vinegar.
  Let the pieces soak in the mixture
  for about 10 seconds, then remove
  and set aside. In another bowl,
  mix the onion, tomato, and $2/3$
  of the basil.

- Add the bread and gently mix the whole thing. Add the rest of the vinegar, the oil, and the salt and pepper.

- Mix well but gently so as not to crumble the bread any further. Top with the rest of the basil. Cover with clear plastic wrap and refrigerate. Serve cold.

- Serves 4.

Uova al Pomodoro

(Eggs and Tomatoes)

When I was growing up during the '50s and '60s, life was less complicated. Surrounding my apartment building were plenty of farms. Going to them to shop for fresh produce was my favorite (and easiest) chore. And I was always sent out for fresh ingredients when my mother was going to make this dish.

INGREDIENTS

4 eggs, beaten

8-10 ripe tomatoes (place in boiling water for 20-30 seconds to remove skin)

2 cups whole fresh basil leaves

1 large red onion, coarsely chopped

2 Tbsp. olive oil

salt and pepper to taste

PREPARATION

- In a deep frying pan, sauté the onion until translucent. Coarsely chop the peeled tomatoes and cook on medium heat for 20 minutes. Add the salt and pepper and the eggs. Mix well.

- Lower the heat and keep stirring to prevent the mixture from sticking to the bottom of the pan. Cook for about 5 minutes or until the egg is cooked, then add the basil and turn off the heat right away. Do not overcook or it will dry up.

- Serve hot.

- Serves 4 to 6.

NOTE: *It's not necessary to have farm-fresh eggs or freshly picked tomatoes. But fresh basil—as opposed to dried—and red onions are a must. Buon appetito!*

KEEP IT SIMPLE

When entertaining, don't take on too much work. Remember, good friends, good wine, and a warm atmosphere go a long way.

CHAPTER THREE

A lire saved is a lire earned...

Survivors of World War II are frugal people, and my mother is no exception. One way she shows this is by always defending her own best interests when it comes to dealing with merchants. I've seen her do it many, many times.

Rancid oil

Once my mother bought a bottle of green extra virgin olive oil from a merchant she'd known for years. When she and my father ate their salad that night, they could taste that the oil was rancid. Next morning she rode the bus for a quarter of an hour clutching that bottle of olive oil and burning with the desire to right the wrong that had been done.

When Mafalda confronted the merchant, he claimed she didn't buy rancid oil from him. They argued back and forth until he said, "Fine, I'll refund your money. But you owe me a thousand lire for the portion you used."

My mother walked next door to the produce store to find out how much her lettuce had cost. When she returned to the merchant, she said, "I owe you a thousand lire for the oil I used, but you owe me two thousand lire for the lettuce that was ruined!"

Chestnuts

Another time, my mother roasted chestnuts for my father and they tasted bad. My mother tried to return the bag of chestnuts to the shopkeeper but he wouldn't take them back, claiming there was nothing wrong with his chestnuts. They argued—and finally my mother called the marketplace *polizia*. The constable reached his hand deep into the shopkeeper's barrel of chestnuts and declared that the bottom was very hot—the chestnuts were fermenting. He made the merchant get rid of the whole lot and give my mother her money back.

Spongecake

Yet another time, my mother realized that when she bought spongecake, the bakery clerk always weighed it with

a piece of cardboard underneath. One day she'd had enough. "*Signorina,*" she said loudly enough for all to hear. "Will you please put my spongecake on a tissue paper when you weigh it? That cardboard probably costs me 300 lire and I'm not buying any cardboard. I'm buying spongecake."

Though my mother liked to go to the bakery, she sometimes made her own desserts—and these we looked forward to immensely. I particularly remember **Paste con Crema Chantilly (Cream Puffs with Chantilly Cream), Zuppa Inglese (English Cake), Jam Crostata (Criss-Cross Cake), Crema Caramellata (Crème Caramel),** and **Torta di Zucca Gialla alla Fiorentina (Pumpkin Pie Florentine Style).**

The fishmonger

I remember seeing how the local fishmonger would shake when he saw my mother coming. Apparently, she had once returned already-cooked red snapper to him (transporting it on the bus, of course) to show him that it smelled like ammonia. Rather than experience that again, this shopkeeper always steered my mother to the freshest fish.

I once saw him take her by the shoulders and say, "No, you don't want that fish. This here is much better!"

When people ask my mother how she could spend so much time on these matters, she replies, "I may be old, but I'm not stupid."

Paste con Crema Chantilly

(Cream Puffs with Chantilly Cream)

This is the type of dish that people still rave about years later. Vinsanto wine accompanies this dessert nicely.

INGREDIENTS

Batter:

$1/2$ cup milk

$1/2$ cup water

$1/2$ cup sweet butter

$1/4$ tsp. salt

1 tsp. sugar

1 cup flour, sifted

4 eggs

Cream:

2 egg yolks

1 tsp. pure vanilla extract

10 Tbsp. sugar

2 Tbsp. flour

2 cups milk (more if necessary)

1 Tbsp. rum

$1/4$ tsp. salt

1 pint heavy cream

PREPARATION

For the batter:

- Place the milk and water in a saucepan over low heat; add the butter and bring to a boil.

- Add the salt, sugar, and sifted flour; keep stirring until the mixture turns into a stiff batter; it will pull away from the pan sides easily.

- Let cool. When cooled, add eggs one at a time, stirring all the while, until all the eggs are incorporated and the batter is fairly smooth.

- Preheat the oven to 350° F., grease a baking sheet with some butter, and place teaspoonfuls of the batter on the baking sheet until all the batter is used up. Make sure to leave space between the dollops of batter—at least 1 $1/2$ inches.

- Raise the oven temperature to 400° just as you put the puffs in; this helps them rise quickly without burning and bake through without drying out. Bake for 20 minutes or until the cream puffs double in size and are golden brown. Turn off the oven, open the door, and let them dry inside the oven for a while.

For the cream:

- In a bowl, mix well with an electric mixer the following: the egg yolks, 1

cup of the milk, 4 Tbsp. of the sugar, and the vanilla, flour, salt, and rum. Start cooking this crème over low heat and, as it thickens, slowly add more milk, mixing continuously. Be sure to add the milk gradually, to get a good creamy consistency. Set aside to cool completely.

- In a large bowl, mix the heavy cream and the remaining 6 Tbsp. of sugar. Beat with an electric beater until the mixture gets fluffy and light.

- Add the heavy cream mixture to the previously made crème slowly and gently. Carefully fold using an upward motion until the two mixtures combine well. Set aside in the refrigerator, covered, for an hour.

- Filling the cream puffs: Cut the cream puffs in half horizontally and fill each with the crema chantilly. Replace the tops. Place on a serving dish and sprinkle with the powdered sugar. Cover and keep refrigerated until ready to serve.

- Serves 4 to 6.

Zuppa Inglese

(English Cake)

When I was a kid, I didn't like this dessert—but my sister did. And that drove me crazy. She would take a piece and flaunt how much she was enjoying it. And I just couldn't join in. Now that I'm an adult, I like it a lot and can't imagine what my problem was!

INGREDIENTS

1 package hard ladyfingers (Savoiardi is the brand used in Italy but you can use whatever you find in the supermarkets here)

2 egg yolks

1 quart milk

4 Tbsp. Nutella chocolate or 2 Tbsp. dark unsweetened cocoa (optional)

2 ¹/₂ Tbsp. cornstarch

3 Tbsp. sugar

2 slivers lemon rind

¹/₂ tsp. pure vanilla extract

pinch of salt

1 cup Maraschino, Grand Marnier, or Strega liqueur

1 cup water

PREPARATION

- Bring the milk to a boil, add the lemon rind pieces, and cook on medium heat for 5 minutes.

- Beat the egg yolks with the vanilla and the sugar; add 1 cup of the hot milk and the cornstarch. Mix well, making sure that the batter doesn't ball up. Add the rest of the hot milk, mix well again, and put back on the stove. Cook for 5 or 6 minutes on low heat. If the cream is too thick, add more milk and mix well.

- Divide the cream in two parts. In one part add the Nutella or dark, unsweetened cocoa if you decide to use it; leave the other part as it is.

- In a bowl, mix the chosen liqueur with water and set aside.

- Now you're going to make layers. Start dipping the ladyfingers in the liqueur–water mix, and lay them evenly in a medium bowl. Spread a layer of the white cream, repeat a layer of the ladyfingers and then cream again (alternating with the dark cream if using). You can dip some of the ladyfingers in espresso coffee for an added flavor.

- When all the ladyfingers and cream are arranged in layers, refrigerate for at least two hours. Then with a dish on top of the bowl, quickly turn the bowl upside down. The English cake should be formed now in the shape of the bowl. Refrigerate again. Serve cold.

- Serves 6.

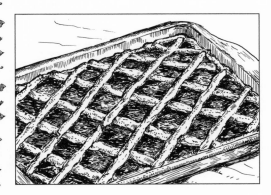

Jam Crostata

(Criss-Cross Cake)

The crosshatch pattern of jam crostata is a familiar sight in Florentine homes. It's a great family treat. Choose any jam you like. The layer of jam should be about ¹/₄ inch thick all around. I like to use wild berries like blackberries, raspberries, and—my personal favorite—elderberries. All of these are tart, a taste that contrasts well with the sweet dough. To this day, crostata reminds me of berry picking with my mother. When we'd picked enough, we'd come back to the house to make jam. My job was to strain the cooked berries, trying to get rid of most of the seeds. It was a little stressful to do under the watchful eyes of my mother. My reward came when Mafalda would offer me a spoonful of jam straight from the pot and watch for my reaction. She always trusted my sense of taste, and a smile from me told her all she needed to know.

INGREDIENTS

4 cups flour

¹⁄₂ lb. butter

1 lb. of your favorite store-bought or homemade jam

3 eggs (2 beaten in one bowl, 1 set aside)

1 cup sugar

pinch of salt

2 Tbsp. Vinsanto (a typical Tuscan sweet wine used with desserts or alone after meals) or rum

PREPARATION

• In a bowl, let the butter soften at room temperature. Add the flour and with a wooden spoon start to incorporate gently the butter with the flour. When incorporated, add the 2 eggs, Vinsanto or rum, sugar, and pinch of salt. Combine everything gently (note: don't work this dough too much because it will tend to burn easily if you do), then set aside to rest for 15 minutes at room temperature.

• Divide the dough in half; get 2 sheets of wax paper ready. Place one sheet on a flat surface and put half of the dough on it. Then put the other sheet of wax paper on top, and start spreading the dough with a rolling pin. The dough should be about ¹⁄₄ inch thick and placed in a baking tray that is 1" deep, 15" long, and 10" wide..

• Take the top layer of wax paper off, turn an ungreased baking pan upside down, and place it on top of the dough. Gently lift the bottom wax paper to help you put the dough in the baking pan. (This type of dough is very delicate, making it hard to handle, but the wax paper helps.)

• Once the dough is in the baking pan, pinch the edges to form a raised crust all around. Spread your favorite jam evenly and set aside.

• Get the other half of the dough and cut a piece about the size of a golf ball. Start working it between the palms of your hands to make it into a long breadstick-like shape, about ¹⁄₂ inch in diameter. Continue cutting pieces the size of golf balls and then making these long shapes until you have used all the dough.

- Get the baking pan with the prepared dough and jam and start placing the long strips diagonally side to side, overlapping one another. Push gently where the strips overlap so they stick together.

- Continue until the whole crosshatch pattern is complete. (See illustration.)

- Beat the remaining egg and brush the top of the dough all around. This will give a shine to the dough when baking.

- Preheat the oven to 300° F. and bake until golden brown, approximately 20 to 25 minutes. Check from time to time because this dough acquires the desired color quickly.

- Serve cold the next day. This dessert gets better as the days go by. You can store it in the refrigerator for a week.

Crema Caramellata

(Crème Caramel)

I was in the mood for a different kind of dessert recently, so I called Mafalda in Florence and asked her how to make crème caramel. I then made it exactly as she said, and believe me, it was superb. I've had this dish in restaurants, but their versions don't come close to this one.

INGREDIENTS

1 quart milk

5 eggs

pinch of salt

8 heaping Tbsp. sugar

¹/₄ tsp. pure vanilla extract

3 strips lemon peel

PREPARATION

For the caramel:

- Put 4 Tbsp. of sugar in a small pan over low heat and bring to a boil, until it starts getting a golden brown color. Be careful not to cook too long because the sugar will burn easily. Keep stirring until color is achieved.

- Quickly pour into a smooth (as opposed to ridged), high-walled metal baking form (can be purchased in a kitchenware shop), making sure that all of the sides and bottom are covered by the melted sugar. Immerse the mold into cold water quickly so the sugar cracks all around. Make sure water doesn't get inside the form. Set aside.

For the crème and the cooking:

- Beat the eggs and sugar; add vanilla and salt. Set aside.

- In a pot, bring all the milk with the lemon peel to a boil; cook for 10

minutes. Take the lemon peel out and discard. Set aside to completely cool.

- Once cooled, add the egg mixture, and mix with an electric beater to make sure all the ingredients are well blended.

- Pour all of the above into the smooth form; place in a double boiler (see note below) and cook in the oven (preheated to 300° F.) for 2 hours or until the top turns golden brown.

- Place in the refrigerator for about 2 hours. Take out and with a flat spatula gently separate the edges from the metal form. Place a plate on top of the form, and with a quick flip of the wrist, turn upside down. If you have separated the edges properly, the crème caramel should slide onto the plate easily. Make sure all the juices and melted sugar are on top. Refrigerate.

- Serve cold.

- Serves 4 to 6.

NOTE: *A double boiler is a metal pan with high walls and no handles in which the form with the crème caramel can fit comfortably. Cold water is then added inside the pan just below the top of the form (making sure no water gets inside with the crème caramel), so that the form is almost floating in water. The water will become hot in the oven. The water actually cooks the crème caramel, giving it a delicate texture and flavor.*

Torta di Zucca Gialla alla Fiorentina

(Pumpkin Pie Florentine Style)

I must have been about 12 years old, and autumn was approaching. The orange pumpkins were ready for harvesting and my mother and I set out to pick a few at a nearby farm. We walked around the pumpkin patch for a long time and finally found only two perfect ones—a small one and a large one. After Mafalda argued with the owner about the price, we set out for home. I volunteered to carry the large one because I was at that age when boys want to prove their strength—and their good manners.

In a little while, though, I needed to sit down on the banks of the Mugnone Stream. My mother wasn't tired, so I told her to wait at the bottom of the stream bank and I'd be there shortly. As I sat, I thought, "Why should I carry this heavy pumpkin down a steep slope when I could just roll it?" So roll it I did. But it picked up speed—and to my horror was heading straight to where my mother was sitting. It hit her with great force on her back. I remember thinking, "I have killed my mama."

But she was okay, though short of breath for a while. I begged her forgiveness but to my surprise she wasn't even angry at me! She just wanted to get home to start making this pumpkin dessert.

INGREDIENTS

2 lbs. pumpkin flesh

2 cups whole milk

1 cup blanched almonds, roasted
in a preheated oven at 200° F.
until golden brown

2 cups sugar

2 cups raisins

1 1/2 cups plain breadcrumbs

4 eggs, lightly beaten

pinch of salt

1/2 tsp. cinnamon powder

6-8 drops pure vanilla extract

4 Tbsp. butter

1/2 tsp. lemon zest

powdered sugar

PREPARATION

- Using a large, heavy knife, cut the pumpkin in half lengthwise. With a spoon, scoop out the seeds and stringy pulp. Slice the pumpkin 6 more times until you have 8 lengthwise pieces. Peel the rind off the pieces. Then cut each pumpkin slice into 6 small chunks.

- With the help of a food processor, carefully putting the pieces in a few at a time, chop until very fine. The chopped pumpkin will be quite moist. Place the pumpkin in a clean kitchen cloth or in a piece of cheesecloth and squeeze out as much water as possible. By the time you finish squeezing the water, the pumpkin will be half what it was. You must get the water out.

- Place the pumpkin in a pot with the milk; simmer (below the boiling point) for about 30 to 45 minutes. Set aside until completely cooled.

- In the food processor, purée the almonds, 1 cup of the breadcrumbs, salt, cinnamon, and sugar. Add this to the chopped pumpkin with the eggs, the raisins, the lemon zest, and the vanilla extract. Mix well with a wooden spoon until nice and smooth. Set aside.

- Using nonstick cooking spray, coat the inside of a high-walled baking mold, making sure not to miss any spots. This is very important because the mix will stick easily to any missed spots. Add the rest of the breadcrumbs. Rotate the mold back and forth to coat thoroughly with the breadcrumbs.

- Gently pour the mix into the mold using a large spoon to scrape the pot. Sprinkle the top with some of the breadcrumbs to prevent the top from burning.

- Preheat the oven to 350° F. and bake for about 1 ½ hours or until the top turns golden brown and cracks.

- Let cool completely. Then place a dish on top, quickly flip it over, and the finished pie will fall onto the dish like magic. Pull off the baking mold, sprinkle with powdered sugar, and serve at room temperature.

- Serves 6 to 8.

A SOPHISTICATED PALATE

The best way to acquire one is to spend a lot of time with people who really know what good food is. I acquired my taste from my mother—who else?

CHAPTER FOUR

Oh, bountiful earth...

Another way my mother showed her frugality was by taking advantage of free food—anywhere and any way she could come by it.

Toward the end of World War II, when food was scarce, she would go to abandoned farms to see what she could find. She sometimes came home loaded with potatoes and sometimes cauliflower. The potatoes could hold for a while, but my mother had to move quickly with the cauliflower. She developed a recipe she calls **Cavolo Ubriaco (Drunken Cauliflower)**, which can be made with red or white wine.

Oooh, radicchio

Accepting nature's generosity whenever she could was a habit my mother found hard to break. Once when she and my father were here in the United States in early spring visiting us, we took a bus tour to Mount Vernon, George Washington's home in Virginia. When my mother saw young dandelion plants growing on the lawn of the historic estate, she broke into a run.

"Ooooooh," she called out. "Radicchio, radicchio." Before we knew it, she was on her knees digging up the young plants.

A park service guard appeared.

"Ma'am," he said politely. "Could you please tell me what you're doing?"

Before waiting for an answer, he explained that she could not dig on land owned by the federal government. When my wife Anna translated this for her, she said, "*Scusi, scusi...*" and wiped the dirt off her hands.

Anna and I never did figure out how she was planning to cook those tender green leaves in her hotel room.

Crabapples

In summers past, my family and I would rent a cottage in upstate New York, and when my parents were visiting, they would come with us. I remember once we were driving on one of the country roads when my mother shouted, "Stop! Oh, my God. Stop!"

I stopped, and my mother jumped out of the car and began picking up crabapples from underneath trees. She didn't care how dirty or how tiny they were—this was free food from Mother Nature and she wasn't about to pass it up. Back at the cottage, she baked a cake with crabapple filling and used the rest of the apples for jelly. No complaints from us.

Elderberries

Another summer, during a stay at the same cottage, we visited an antiques shop housed in a large barn. My mother's curiosity—about food—got the best of her when she saw one of the owners at the counter sorting berries.

"What are those? What is he doing?" She kept nudging Anna. Finally, Anna agreed to translate so that Mafalda and the antiques dealer could talk. Mafalda learned that the mystery berries were called elderberries (new to her), and joy of all joys, they were growing just up the road!

Of course, we had to go right then. Elderberries are very dark red and grow on a beautiful tall bush. My mother fell in love. We picked and picked, carrying Mafalda's treasure off in t-shirts, jackets, and whatever else we could rummage from the car. When we got back to the cottage, she made elderberry jam.

Raspberries

When we weren't traveling upstate, my mother took advantage of the glorious bounty provided by the rich lands and seas of Eastern Long Island, where we are very fortunate to live.

Early one morning, I thought it might be nice to take Mafalda and Renato, my father, raspberry picking right here in our little village of Wading River. Mafalda dressed seriously for this event. She emerged from her room in protective clothing from head to toe. Raspberries grow on a very thorny bush, after all.

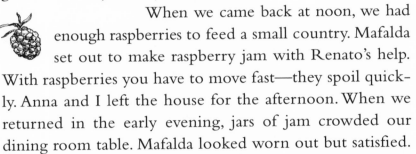 When we came back at noon, we had enough raspberries to feed a small country. Mafalda set out to make raspberry jam with Renato's help. With raspberries you have to move fast—they spoil quickly. Anna and I left the house for the afternoon. When we returned in the early evening, jars of jam crowded our dining room table. Mafalda looked worn out but satisfied.

"You should have seen this place a few hours ago," she exclaimed as a greeting. She went on to explain how the kitchen counters, the kitchen floor, the stove, and the sink had all been stained pink by the raspberries. It was only with very hard work and a can of Ajax that the two of them had been able to return our kitchen to its previous state. Anna breathed a sigh of relief and thought, "Well, at least this is over with."

She was wrong. The next morning, Mafalda announced that she wanted to go raspberry picking again. She repeated the entire previous day's events—the picking, the making

of the jam, the staining of the kitchen, and the cleaning up afterwards.

That's the way my mother is. There's no thought of "Let's leave some raspberries on the bush for somebody else." No way.

Seafood

In those days, my mother always took advantage of the fact that Long Island is surrounded by water. "Where there's water, there are creatures that live in water," was her thinking. At a nearby inlet, Mafalda would wade through low tide to scoop up mussels. These treasures she took back to our house, scrubbed, and used for the astonishingly delicious dish we call **Cozze Ripiene (Stuffed Mussels)**.

For some reason, my mother never learned to swim. But that didn't stop her from going out on my boat whenever I decided to fish on Long Island Sound, which is right at the end of our road. She didn't mind clouds, she didn't mind wind. She was intent on catching fish.

Whenever she caught one, she smiled like a child. But once I made her frown. She caught a bluefish that was too small and I asked her to throw it back. She refused. I told her it was illegal to keep them when they're too young. In response, she clenched the fish between her knees. It wriggled and squirmed.

I could not get her to throw the fish back. I guess it went against her reasoning, which was, "When nature gives, take it and run."

We always eat well when my mother visits us here on Eastern Long Island. She's especially fond of the fresh lobster available and has frequently made her outstanding ***Sugo d'Aragosta alla Mafalda (Lobster Sauce Mafalda Style)*** for us.

She also loves the ubiquitous farm stands this area is known for. We live near an especially large and wonderful one (housed in an enormous barnlike structure) called Lewin Farms. Lewin Farms is a real working farm that produces tons of vegetables. Next time you buy potatoes at the supermarket, take a look and see if they're from Lewin Farms!

During her summer visits, my mother would always insist on going to Lewin to stock up on the nutritious summer squash. When she did, we were treated to ***Zucchini Ripiene (Stuffed Zucchini Squash),*** and ***Zucchini al Limone (Zucchini with Lemon Sauce).***

GARLIC

When buying garlic, make sure it's hard. If it feels squishy, it's going to sprout soon. Keep garlic in a dry, dark place. The vegetable drawer of your refrigerator is okay, but don't let the garlic get moist.

Cavolo Ubriaco

(Drunken Cauliflower)

My mother makes this recipe with white wine but I make it with red because it has more punch to it. This dish is a real hit at get-togethers at my house because it's delicious—and a conversation piece.

INGREDIENTS

1/4 cup extra virgin olive oil

6 cloves garlic (or to taste), peeled and crushed

1 medium-sized cauliflower

2 sprigs fresh rosemary, cut into pieces

salt and pepper to taste

1 cup dry red wine

PREPARATION

- Cut the cauliflower into florets, discarding the central stem. In a wok (if not available, use a large nonstick pan), place the olive oil, garlic, cauliflower, and rosemary.

- Over medium-high heat, cook the florets until they turn medium dark brown. Stir gently with a wooden spoon or flip the pan to get all sides to brown. (Keep the florets whole as much as possible.)

- When the cauliflower turns medium dark brown, add salt and pepper. Remove the pan from the heat and add the red wine. Return the pan to the heat and continue tossing or stirring gently until the wine is completely absorbed, about 4 to 5 minutes.

- Serves 4 to 6.

FAMILY FIRST

As Aunt Rina always used to say, never make a recipe for the first time for guests.

Cozze Ripiene

(Stuffed Mussels)

Besides being delicious, this dish brings back a childhood memory for me. My mother always asked me to tie the mussels together with thread. It was a delicate operation and I should have been flattered she entrusted it to me. But, being a kid, I looked upon it as a chore. Not anymore!

INGREDIENTS

3 lbs. whole fresh mussels (scrubbed well outside and inside after opening on flat side of mussel)

2 cups milk

$^1/_2$ lb. mortadella, finely chopped

1 lb. stale bread soaked in the 2 cups of milk for 10 min. (squeeze excess milk and set aside)

1 16-oz. can crushed tomatoes

$^1/_2$ cup chopped fresh Italian parsley

2-3 cloves garlic, peeled and chopped

$^1/_2$ cup grated romano cheese

pinch of nutmeg

$^1/_4$ lb. lean ground beef

$^1/_4$ lb. boiled chicken, finely chopped

1 large onion, chopped

salt and pepper to taste

4 Tbsp. butter or margarine ($^1/_2$ stick)

PREPARATION

- Make a mixture of the following ingredients: mortadella, soaked bread, parsley, cheese, garlic, nutmeg, ground beef, boiled chicken. Mix all very well. Set aside. Fill every mussel with the mixture (do not overfill) and tie each one closed with white sewing thread (you don't want colored thread in your food). When finished, set aside.

- Prepare the tomato sauce: Sauté the onion in the butter; add tomatoes, and cook for 10–15 minutes. If there is any of the stuffing for the mussels left over, add it to the tomato sauce.

- Add the filled mussels and cook on medium heat for not more than 15 minutes, stirring occasionally. Serve hot.

- Serves 4.

Sugo D'Aragosta alla Mafalda

(Lobster Sauce Mafalda Style)

I have a friend who is a lobsterman and sometimes I do mechanical work on his boat for him. I won't accept money but often he rewards me with lobsters. Once, when my mother was visiting, I came home with two dozen. My mother took one look at them and a light bulb seemed to go on in her head. Within minutes (it seemed), she had prepared this wonderful dish—and received raves from all of us. Now that I know how much my mother likes lobsters, I sometimes freeze lobster meat (after parboiling) and take it to her when I visit Italy. She considers it such a treasure that I think the lobster still sits in her freezer awaiting a special occasion!

INGREDIENTS

1 $\frac{1}{2}$ to 2 lb. whole fresh lobster

2 cloves garlic, minced

1 cup finely minced fresh parsley

$\frac{1}{2}$ tsp. peperoncino (hot red pepper)

1 large Knorr beef bouillon cube

1 cup dry white wine

1 tsp. flour

1 cup heavy cream (can substitute half-and-half or plain milk)

salt to taste

PREPARATION

- Fill a large pot with water, bring it to a boil, and put the lobster in. Cover and cook for 5 to 10 minutes or until the lobster turns bright red. Take out the lobster and use only the claws and tail. Cut the claws and tail in pieces no bigger than a dime; set aside.

- Put the garlic, parsley, hot red pepper, bouillon, and white wine in a medium pot. Cook for 5 minutes.

- In a medium bowl, mix the flour and heavy cream well, making sure the flour doesn't bunch up into little balls. Then add this to the garlic, parsley, hot red pepper, bouillon, and white wine. Cook for another 5 minutes, stirring constantly. Add the lobster; bring to a near boil and take off the stove. Keep warm until serving time.

- Great over any type of pasta, but spaghetti is the best in my opinion.

- Serves 4 to 6.

NOTE: *Never reboil lobster—it will get hard. Just keep it warm.*

Zucchini Ripiene

(Stuffed Zucchini Squash)

My mother would make this dish using the round zucchini found in Florence. You can use the cylindrical zucchini found in this country with no problem. What I like about this dish is that nothing gets thrown out. You core out the zucchini and then use the pulp in the stuffing.

INGREDIENTS

6 zucchini, about 1 $\frac{1}{2}$ to 2 inches in diameter

4 fresh Italian sausages (any flavor), casings removed

1 small onion, finely chopped and sautéed in a little olive oil

1 clove garlic, finely chopped

2 Tbsp. finely chopped fresh parsley

$\frac{1}{2}$ cup grated romano cheese

1 egg, beaten

2 slices mortadella, finely chopped

salt and pepper to taste

4 Tbsp. salted butter ($\frac{1}{2}$ stick)

PREPARATION

- Cut each zucchini in half lengthwise and hollow out the pulp with a small knife or spoon. Set the pulp aside.

- In a bowl, mix the sausage with the sautéed onion, garlic, parsley, cheese, mortadella, egg, and salt and pepper. Add the zucchini pulp. Mix well using your hands, then stuff each zucchini.

- Put the butter in a small baking dish and place in the oven at 350° F. until the butter is melted and turning golden in color. Arrange the zucchini one next to the other, stuffed side up, leaving some space in between. Cook for about an hour or until the zucchini starts changing to a golden brown color. Keep basting with the juices while it cooks. Do not turn them over.

- Serve hot. Could be a main dish or an accompaniment to meat or poultry.

- Serves 4 to 6.

Zucchini al Limone

(Zucchini with Lemon Sauce)

Some people can't see how zucchini works with lemon. (My son, Simon, a zucchini hater since birth, can't see how zucchini works with anything!) But this dish is actually delicious. For the zucchini lovers among us, try this, you'll like it. It's a unique dish I learned from my mother (who else?).

INGREDIENTS

2 lbs. small fresh zucchini (not larger than ³/₄ inch in diameter and 8-10 inches long)

INGREDIENTS
Fresh is best—always.

4 Tbsp. sweet butter (¹/₂ stick)

4 cups oil for frying

2 lemons, squeezed (use the juice and the pulp)

4-6 fresh mint leaves, chopped

salt and freshly ground pepper to taste

PREPARATION

- Wash the zucchini well and cut into slices (the round way) ¹/₄ to ³/₈ inch thick. Set aside.

- In a frying pan, add the oil over medium-high heat. When the oil is hot, add 2 handfuls of sliced zucchini and fry them until they turn dark golden brown. Take them out and set aside over paper towels to absorb the excess oil. Repeat with the rest of the zucchini.

- In a medium-sized pot, melt the butter and add the zucchini and the mint. Quickly sauté over medium-high heat for 3 minutes. Add the lemon; stir and serve with freshly ground pepper and salt to taste. Serve hot.

- Great as a side dish with fish or poultry.

- Serves 4.

CHAPTER FIVE

"Divina Provvidenza"
(or, what the cat dragged in...)

Growing up, I would often hear stories of what life had been like during World War II, when food was scarce and meat was scarcer—you just couldn't get it. One of my favorite stories was about the day my mother's cat (she had lots of them over the years) came home with a present—a big steak gripped in its teeth. The cat's name was Musetta, which means "little face." My mother grabbed the steak from Musetta's little face—and her own face lit up.

Mafalda washed the meat carefully, cut it up, and made a stew with potatoes, onions, and carrots. Always fair, my mother took a piece of the cooked meat and fed it to Musetta—who was, after all, the heroine of the day.

Musetta must have liked the queenly treatment, because she came back with another steak a few weeks later. Mafalda knew the steaks were coming from someone's windowsill (there was no refrigeration in those days) and that they would be missing them. But she rationalized that the meat came from "some fascist big shot in the government" anyway, so she didn't feel so bad.

When this new steak presented itself once more by feline delivery, my mother again washed the meat, cooked it, and served it.

"Ahhh," she said, looking at the meal laid out on the kitchen table. "*Divina Provvidenza*. That's what this is!" Somehow I think of it more as "what the cat dragged in."

We weren't always struggling for food during the years I was growing up in Florence. After the war, there was more money and more food available. My mother enjoyed selecting meats at the butcher and coming home to fix a nice dinner for us. A meal she made often, and which was very much appreciated by my father and my sister and me, is **Scaloppine alla Livornese (Chops Livornese Style).** Other meat dishes that met with our approval then—and still do now, with my own family—are *Involtini alla* 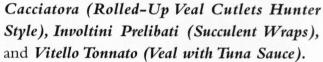 *Cacciatora (Rolled-Up Veal Cutlets Hunter Style), Involtini Prelibati (Succulent Wraps),* and *Vitello Tonnato (Veal with Tuna Sauce).*

Scaloppine alla Livornese

(Chops Livornese Style)

This dish is easy to make, and therefore always a success.

INGREDIENTS

6 cloves garlic (or to taste), peeled and crushed

1/4 cup olive oil

4 medium-sized, 1/2-inch-thick lamb chops (boneless), veal chops (boneless), or center-cut pork chops with bone removed (buy good quality meat for this recipe)

4 Tbsp. flour

1 28-oz. can crushed tomatoes

10 fresh sage leaves, 6 tied together and 4 reserved for garnish (if fresh sage leaves are not available, substitute 1 tsp. powdered sage)

salt and pepper to taste

PREPARATION

- In a large frying pan over low heat, sauté the garlic in the oil until golden brown. Remove the pan from the heat for a moment. Remove the garlic— you will use it again later.

- Rinse the chops and pat them dry. Place the flour on a plate and dip the chops into it, coating both sides.

- Brown the chops on both sides in the garlic-flavored oil over medium heat. Transfer the chops to a plate; cover to keep warm.

- Lower the heat and to the same oil add the crushed tomatoes, the 6 tied sage leaves or powdered sage, reserved garlic, salt and pepper. Simmer for about 10 minutes, stirring occasionally.

- Remove the tied sage leaves if fresh ones were used, and spoon about a cupful of the mixture into a frying pan large enough to hold the meat. Place the chops on top of the sauce and pour the remaining sauce over them. Cover and cook for 10 minutes over low heat.

- Place the chops in a serving dish, using fresh sage for garnish. Leftover sauce can be spooned over pasta.

- Serve hot.

- Serves 4.

TO SAUTÉ GARLIC AND ONIONS

Always sauté the onion first! Wait until the onion is translucent and then add the garlic to the pan. If you put them in at the same time, the garlic will burn.

Involtini alla Cacciatora

(Rolled-Up Veal Cutlets Hunter Style)

My mother would make this whenever she came across some nice veal at the store— and we rejoiced when she did. Why is it called hunter style? My mother's guess is that it's a quick way to make something tasty— and that's what hunters do when they have to take care of their own meals.

INGREDIENTS

1 lb. veal cutlets, tenderized to ¼ inch thick and about 4 x 4 inches square

¼ lb. chicken livers, cut into pieces

1 oz. prosciutto, shredded

2 Tbsp. butter

3 Tbsp. olive oil

1 green scallion, finely chopped

½ cup Marsala (a sweet Sicilian wine that is widely available)

1 cup chicken broth

1 tsp. finely chopped fresh sage

2 Tbsp. finely chopped parsley

½ tsp. salt

½ tsp. freshly ground pepper

1 cup flour

PREPARATION

- Sauté the chicken livers in the oil, remove, and set aside.

- In the same oil, sauté the prosciutto and the scallion; add the sage, parsley, salt and pepper, then return the livers to this mixture. Mix well and set aside.

- Place the veal cutlets on a flat surface. Put 2 Tbsp. of the mixture in the middle of a cutlet, then roll it up, keeping it closed at the ends with one or two toothpicks. Repeat this for all the cutlets. Roll them in the flour.

- In a skillet, sauté the rolled-up cutlets in butter, then remove. Add the Marsala and the broth and bring to a boil; cook for about a minute.

- Return the cutlets and cook for 15 minutes at medium heat.

- Serve hot.

- Serves 4 to 6.

Involtini Prelibati

(Succulent Wraps)

Some people shy away from liver (I don't know why), but if you want something very tasty, put it in. This dish has a lot of character and will impress guests as well as your own family. What's different about it is that you serve it cold.

INGREDIENTS

6 thin veal or pork cutlets

$^1/_4$ lb. prosciutto

$^1/_4$ lb. ground pork

15 chicken livers
(optional, but do it!)

3 eggs

6 fresh sage leaves, or $^1/_2$ tsp. dried

4 Tbsp. butter ($^1/_2$ stick)

2 Tbsp. chopped parsley

1 cup grated parmigiano cheese

$^1/_2$ cup plain breadcrumbs

1 cup dry white wine

$^1/_4$ cup olive oil

1 cup chicken or beef broth

salt and pepper to taste

1 package unflavored gelatin

PREPARATION

- Place the ground pork, the prosciutto, and the chicken livers in a food processor and process for one minute. Put the mixture in a bowl with the parsley, parmigiano cheese, breadcrumbs, eggs, and salt and pepper. Mix well. Set aside.

- Flatten out the 6 cutlets; fill each one with the mixture and roll up like a cannelloni. Keep it from unrolling with one toothpick at each end.

- Using the olive oil and the butter and adding the sage leaves or dried sage, sauté the rolled cutlets at medium heat for about 10 minutes, splashing them with the white wine from time to time.

- Add the broth and finish cooking until the broth is evaporated, about 15 or 20 minutes. Let cool.

- Prepare the gelatin according to the instructions. Let it cool off but not harden.

- Meanwhile, slice the meat rolls into medallions about $^1/_2$ inch thick.

- Arrange in a bowl and add the cooled gelatin. Put into the refrigerator and let the gelatin set.

- Serve cold.

- Serves 4 to 6.

Vitello Tonnato

(Veal with Tuna Sauce)

What can I say about this dish? It's simple and it's good.

INGREDIENTS

2 lbs. veal brisket (preferable, but
can substitute beef brisket)

1 can solid white tuna in oil

1 can anchovies (optional)

3 or 4 hard-boiled eggs (use only the yolk)

juice from 2 freshly squeezed lemons

1 lemon, thinly sliced (for garnish)

4 Tbsp. capers (1 Tbsp. reserved
for garnish)

olive oil

PREPARATION

- Cover the brisket in water, bring to a boil, then reduce the heat and simmer until quite tender, approximately 1 1/2 to 2 hours. Check for tenderness from time to time. Set aside to cool.

- Once cooled, cut slices about 3/8 inch thick. Arrange the slices on a platter overlapping each other. Set aside.

- In a blender, blend the tuna (including its oil), hard–boiled egg yolks, lemon juice, 3 Tbsp. capers, and the anchovies (if using). Blend at blending speed and add olive oil a little at a time—enough to make a fairly liquid sauce.

- Pour this sauce over the brisket. Garnish with the remaining capers and lemon slices. Refrigerate.

- Serve cold.

- Serves 6.

ON COOKING SMELLS

This is from Anna: If you have a two-story house, close the bedroom doors upstairs. Cooking smells tend to rise to the occasion.

Venus did what she could to help
make those Chianti wines...

CHAPTER SIX

Treasures from the garden...

If there's one thing I've learned from my mother, it's to value and honor the plants that grow on this earth. When I think of everything I have growing in my backyard here in fertile Eastern Long Island, I have to say I treasure my grapevines and my basil plants the most.

Love affair with the grape

I share my mother's passion not only for food—but also for the grape. My mother would drink wine with her meals but I never saw her get drunk—only happier.

I grow my own grapes on vines that shade the back deck at my home. At the end of the summer, when the grapes are ripe, I make homemade wine and store the bottles in my wine cellar (known as "the basement" to others in my family) for winter consumption. But I also use those freshly picked grapes to make a treat that can be devoured right away. I whip up ***Schiacciata con L'uva (Grape Cake)***, which is a dessert my mother used to bake for me when I was a child.

I indulge in store-bought wines, too. I'd be a fool not to since this part of Long Island, both the North Fork (where I live) and the South Fork (where the rich people live), is becoming known for its vineyards.

From time to time in this book, you'll see mention of Vinsanto, either as an ingredient in a recipe or as an accompaniment to one. Vinsanto is one of my favorites. Translated into English, it means "holy wine." Holy or not, it's delicious! It's a sweet dessert wine that's common in Tuscany. You can find it just about anywhere. Stray toward the high end of the price range—a good Vinsanto is well worth it.

While I'm on the subject of wine, let me put in my two cents about which wines go with which foods. The so-called rule is that you drink white with seafood and red with meat. In Italy, most folks don't necessarily go along with that. If they want to drink red, they drink it. The reasoning behind the rule is that a white wine is more delicate, so you can taste the fish better, and this does make sense. But there are a lot of red wines that are delicate and appropriate, too. That said, I'll leave the research to you. *Salute!*

Ode to basil

I do love my grapes, but if I could only have one type of plant growing in my garden (heaven forbid!), there would be no contest—I'd choose basil. Fresh basil is an absolute must in cooking. Dried basil is as tasteless as sawdust.

I don't believe any other people use basil as extensively as the Italians. My mother and I are forever hooked on this delicious and versatile herb.

Basil belongs to the mint family. It has such a wonderful fragrance and flavor—rich, spicy, mildly peppery, with a trace of mint and clove. Native to India and Asia, it has been cultivated for 5,000 years, and I can see why.

Basil works in practically every Italian dish. Among our family's favorites are **Scaloppine al Basilico (Scaloppini with Basil), Spaghetti a Fiori di Basilico (Spaghetti with Basil Flowers),** and **Involtini di Melanzane alla Mafalda (Eggplant Rollatini Mafalda Style)**. It's almost impossible to overdo your use of it. Besides being the main ingredient in pesto sauce, it can be added to salads, soups, fish, meat, and vegetable dishes easily—and with great results.

Basil in a jar from the supermarket is basil that has lost all its flavor in the drying process. (If you've ever dried basil and it gives off a fragrance, that's it losing its flavor!) I strongly favor freshly picked basil, freshly frozen basil, or ice-cubed basil (see explanation).

I grow my own basil in my herb garden (it's an annual), but it can be bought fresh year round in any good produce store, even in the off-season months.

I even grow basil in the winter. I place basil seeds (which I get by letting some of my plants flower and then collecting the seeds) in a flowerpot and place it by a sunny window. Within weeks I have fresh basil leaves ready to use.

- To freeze fresh basil, pick the leaves, wash them, and dry them well with a paper towel. Then place small portions of them into small zip-locked bags. Place the bags in the freezer and use at your convenience.

- For ice-cubed basil—which can be fun to drop into soups and sauces—pick and wash the basil, place it in a blender, add some water, and puree until smooth. Pour the puréed basil into ice cube trays and let it freeze. Then take them out and wrap each ice cube individually with aluminum foil. Place the wrapped cubes in a plastic bag and keep them in the freezer.

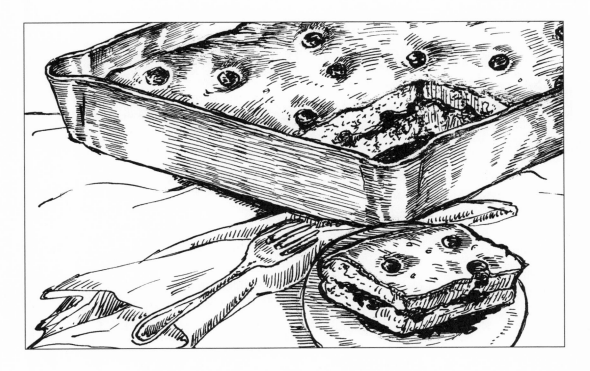

Schiacciata con L'uva

(Grape Cake)

I remember this recipe with distinct pleasure. On some mornings, just before I left for school, my mother would tell me she was going to bake my favorite snack—grape cake—that day. She knew I loved it for its taste, but she also knew it was my favorite because my sister hated it—and that meant I didn't have to share with her!

INGREDIENTS

2 lbs. seedless black grapes
(the darker, the better)

3 $1/2$ cups flour

2 $1/2$ tsp. active dry yeast

11 oz. milk

2 cups plus 2 Tbsp. sugar

6 Tbsp. olive oil

2 tsp. anise seeds

1 tsp. pure vanilla extract

$1/2$ cup sweet wine (Vinsanto is best)

pinch of salt

PREPARATION

- **Yeast starter:** Make your yeast starter by putting the yeast in a small bowl with ½ cup warm milk, 2 Tbsp. sugar, and ½ cup flour. Mix gently with a wooden spoon or a plastic spatula (never use metal) until smooth. Cover with a cloth, set in a warm place and let rise (approximately ½ hour).

- When the yeast starter has risen, mix it in a large bowl with the rest of the flour, 2 Tbsp. oil, salt, and the rest of the milk. Knead it for about ½ hour or until smooth. Set aside covered in a warm location to rise for about 1 ½ hours. It will double in volume.

- Pick 15 or 20 larger grapes from the 2 lbs. and set aside. Put the rest of the grapes in a large bowl and crush them coarsely with your hands. Add the vanilla, the sweet wine, 1 tsp. anise seeds, and 1 cup sugar. Mix well and set aside. Cut the dough in half. Take a half and work it with a wooden dowel to fit a 9 x 12 baking pan (or close to it). Make sure that the dough goes up the sides of the pan.

- Then spread the grape mixture on the dough, juices and all, and set aside. Spread the second half of the dough as before, but smaller, just enough to cover the grapes in the pan. Pinch the two layers of dough together so they stick. Mix the remaining oil and the anise seeds. With a brush, spread it on top of the dough, and sprinkle with the remaining sugar. Take the 15 or 20 grapes saved before and at random gently press into the dough until they are about halfway in.

- Preheat the oven to 350° F. and bake until the top is golden brown (approximately 1 ½ hours).

- Tastes best when still warm from the oven.

Scaloppine al Basilico

(Scaloppini with Basil)

This is a mouth-watering recipe that uses plenty of fresh basil leaves, and you know how I feel about basil.

INGREDIENTS

1 lb. thin veal scaloppini (substitute thin center-cut pork scaloppini, sirloin or filet mignon scaloppini)

1 cup flour

2 large white onions, coarsely chopped

2 cloves garlic, coarsely chopped

$^1/_2$ cup balsamic vinegar

3 cups basil leaves

1 cup extra virgin olive oil

salt and freshly ground pepper to taste

PREPARATION

- Dip the scaloppini into the flour, making sure to coat well. Set aside.

- In a skillet, heat $^1/_2$ cup oil and quickly brown the scaloppini. Take them out of the pan and set aside.

- In the same skillet, heat the rest of the oil and sauté the onions over medium heat until translucent.

- Add the garlic and sauté for another 5 minutes. Add the basil and while stirring add the balsamic vinegar and the salt. Let evaporate at medium heat for 3 to 5 minutes. Pour this mixture into a bowl to be used later.

- Return the scaloppini to the skillet and then pour the onion, garlic, basil, and balsamic vinegar mixture on top.

- Stir and cook for 5 minutes over medium heat.

- Serve hot with freshly ground pepper on top.

- Serves 4.

Spaghetti a Fiori di Basilico

(Spaghetti with Basil Flowers)

I went to the Umbrian town of Piediluco (where my mother was born) several years ago and was talking to my cousin Libero. We got into a conversation about basil—always on the mind of any serious Italian cook—and we are all serious—and he asked what I do with the flowers of the basil plant after I pinch them off. The reason we pinch them off is to keep the plant growing. Once the plant produces a flower, its reason for living is over. So you have to trick it. My answer to my cousin was that I toss the flowers away. He told me I must be out of my mind and promptly gave me this recipe. The flower (as you will see) has a much more pungent taste than the milder leaf. I'll never throw the flowers away again, I promise, cousin.

INGREDIENTS

1 lb. thin spaghetti or capellini

2 Tbsp. basil flowers in bloom, crumbled with your fingers

1/2 cup olive oil

salt

some grated parmigiano cheese

PREPARATION

- In a small pot, heat the olive oil; add the basil flowers. Take the pot off the stove and set aside. Do not cook it any longer—just let it sit.

- Fill a large pot with water, add 2 Tbsp. salt and bring to a boil. Add spaghetti and cook until al dente.

- Drain the spaghetti and then quickly return it to the large pot. Add the olive oil and basil flowers.

- Stir well; sprinkle with parmigiano cheese.

- Serve very hot.

- Serves 4 to 6.

Involtini di Melanzane alla Mafalda

(Eggplant Rollatini Mafalda Style)

Another wonderful basil-intensive dish. Since it requires some work, you might want to double the recipe and use it as a main dish. My mother liked to make this when eggplants were in season in late summer. She always went to the farm next door where they had perfect shiny ones waiting to be bought.

INGREDIENTS

2 lbs. mozzarella cheese, shredded

2 long Italian eggplants, peeled and thinly sliced the long way, about 1/4 to 3/8 inch thick

1/2 lb prosciutto, thinly sliced

1/2 lb. romano cheese, grated

10-20 large fresh basil leaves (equal to the number of eggplant slices)

Basic Basil Tomato Sauce:

1 lb. fresh ripe tomatoes

4 Tbsp. olive oil

salt and pepper to taste

15 fresh basil leaves

PREPARATION

- Grill the peeled eggplant slices on the barbecue to give them a smoky taste. If a barbecue grill is not available, use your oven's broiler.

- Take a slice of eggplant, place some shredded mozzarella cheese in the middle, and roll it. Set aside. Repeat with each of the grilled eggplant slices.

- Place a slice of prosciutto on a flat surface. Place a basil leaf in the center. Place the rolled eggplant over the basil leaf and then sprinkle 1 tsp. grated romano cheese over the eggplant. Roll the prosciutto, with the rolled eggplant inside, gently. Repeat with the rest of the prosciutto and rolled eggplants.

- Put 2 cups of prepared tomato sauce (right) in a baking pan and distribute evenly all around. Arrange the roll-ups in the baking pan one next to the other so they won't unroll. Add more tomato sauce on top of the eggplants, making sure they all have tomato sauce over them. Sprinkle the remaining shredded mozzarella on top.

- Bake the eggplant rollatini in a pre-heated 350° F. oven for 1 hour or until the top starts turning golden brown.

- Serve warm. Sprinkle grated romano cheese on top when serving.

- Serves 4 to 6.

Basic Basil Tomato Sauce:

Take 1 lb. fresh ripe tomatoes (put them in boiling water for 20 to 30 seconds, then peel off the skin), cut them in cubes and set aside. (If fresh tomatoes are not available, a 16-oz. can of crushed tomatoes can be used as a substitute, but fresh is always better.)

- Heat 4 Tbsp. olive oil in a pot, add the tomatoes, salt and pepper, and simmer at medium heat for 10 minutes. Remove from the stove and add basil leaves. Stir well and set aside.

- There is a rule of thumb that must be respected, and Mafalda would be upset if I didn't say it here: You must never, ever cook the basil once you've placed it in the tomato sauce. The heat of the sauce is sufficient to allow the basil to release its natural flavor.

SALT "TO TASTE"

Some chefs are insulted if you salt their food after it's served to you. I think that's silly. You should never be the judge of someone else's taste.

CHAPTER SEVEN

A teenager gets a taste of life...

My teenage summers as Mafalda's son provided me with stories I still tell to this day. She was as strong-willed as ever, and I as eager as any teen to control my own life. I had my triumphs, but I'm sure you can guess who usually got her way! It also won't surprise you that food was almost always part of the story—and the love of a mother for her son always the main ingredient.

Away at the beach...but not far enough

When I was 17, three of my buddies and I went to a beach town called Rimini, where we set up a tent and camped for the summer. We loved being on our own and got to know lots of other teenagers, especially American girls, who always fascinated us. In the midst of all this fun, Mafalda arrived one day out of the blue.

She had been on the train for two and a half hours just to bring food to us. She worried that we wouldn't have enough to eat while camping (we didn't), and she arrived with **Lasagne**, one of the biggest I'd ever seen her make.

My friends and I ate it all up within minutes of her arrival. I think Mafalda got a tiny piece for her efforts. As soon as we ate, I ushered my mother to the exit of the campground and bade her farewell. Lasagne is nice, but freedom is better.

Restaurant school and the angry chef

Another episode from my teenage years gave me a whole new appreciation for my mother's wonderful ways with food—even if it foiled one of her own little schemes to rule my life. At one point (probably when she saw me drifting aimlessly through another summer), Mafalda decided I should go to restaurant school.

In keeping with her newly hatched plan to turn me into a professional cook, she sent me away to a resort—not, to lie in the warm, relaxing sun, but to be on my feet in a hot, steamy kitchen.

What Mafalda didn't know was that all her years of feeding me good food would be her downfall.

Every day when I got hungry, I went across the street to a little pizza place and ate their food. My boss, who was the chef of the resort, wondered why his new kitchen helper was eating elsewhere. Politely, he inquired why. Politely, I told him the food in his kitchen was inedible. He came thundering after me. I never saw anyone so angry! He said later that if he had caught me he would have put me in one of the big, hot bubbling pots on the stove.

It still amazes me to this day that the patrons of this expensive resort never sent the food back. I can't help but think of the joy they'd have felt eating any one of Mafalda's "company" dishes.

If she'd been the chef at this resort, the menu would surely have included *Cannelloni di Crespelle (Crepes Cannelloni), Ravioli Ignudi (Naked Ravioli),* and *Cipolle Gelatinate (Onions in Gelatin).* If sage leaves or truffles were available, *Foglie di Salvia Ripiene (Giant Sage Leaves Stuffed),* and *Spaghetti al Tartufo (Spaghetti with Truffle Sauce)* would have joined the others among the diners' favorites.

I remember Mafalda taking such pride in serving these special dishes to guests at home. She never failed to enjoy hearing their many compliments. I can just picture her going from table to table at this resort, waiting impatiently to hear what everyone had to say!

Lasagne alla Mafalda

(Lasagne Mafalda Style)

Much to everyone's surprise (and probably even yours), there's no ricotta in real Italian lasagne. My mother first encountered ricotta in lasagne during a visit to New York (not at my house), and she was horrified. She pushed her plate away and ate something else instead. I think if I ever used ricotta in lasagne my mother would disown me! But this lasagne of Mafalda's is the real thing, and I know you'll enjoy it.

INGREDIENTS

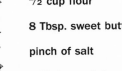

1 lb. lasagne noodles

2 cloves garlic, minced

2 medium onions, chopped

1 lb. ground sirloin

1/2 lb. ground pork

2 Tbsp. minced parsley

1 lb. mozzarella cheese, shredded

4 Tbsp. olive oil

1 1/2 tsp. salt

1/2 tsp. pepper

1 cup fresh basil leaves

2 28-oz. cans crushed tomatoes

1 cup water

1/2 cup grated parmigiano cheese

Béchamel:

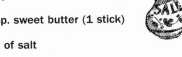

1/2 cup flour

8 Tbsp. sweet butter (1 stick)

pinch of salt

milk (enough to make a liquidy batter)

PREPARATION

For the béchamel:

- In a small pan, melt the stick of butter, then add the flour and salt. Mix well and keep mixing with a wooden spoon until smooth. Cook over low heat until the mixture starts turning light golden brown.

- Start adding the milk slowly, mixing at the same time. Add more milk as the béchamel thickens, and keep on adding and mixing until you get a smooth, not-too-thick consistency (on the liquidy side is preferred).

- Make sure the mixture doesn't stick to the bottom of the pan. Set aside covered.

Lasagne:

- Cook the lasagne noodles in salted boiling water for 15 minutes. Drain and set aside.

- Heat the oil in a skillet and sauté the chopped onion until it turns translucent. Add the minced garlic and sauté a few more minutes, until the garlic starts turning pale brown.

- Add the ground sirloin, ground pork, parsley, salt, and pepper and cook until crumbly and brown. Add the crushed tomatoes and water, and simmer for 10 minutes. Add the basil leaves, remove the skillet from the heat immediately, and set aside.

- Place a thin layer of meat sauce on the bottom of a baking pan large enough to accommodate the lasagne noodles the long way. Stretch a few noodles across to cover the sauce. Place 5 or 6 spoonfuls of the béchamel sauce randomly over the noodles. Then sprinkle some mozzarella over the béchamel. Spread another layer of meat sauce over the mozzarella, then repeat the same layering until most of the ingredients are used up.

- Add any remaining sauce, mozzarella, and béchamel on top. Sprinkle with the parmigiano cheese and bake in a preheated oven at 350° F. for 45 minutes or until the top forms a brown crust. Take it out, cool for 10 minutes and serve.

- Serve warm, not too hot.

- Serves 6 to 8.

Cannelloni di Crespelle

(Crepes Cannelloni)

My mother didn't mind the extra work involved in making these crepes. She usually did it when a special guest was coming for dinner, and she basked in the glow of the compliments she would get.

INGREDIENTS

Crepes:

6 eggs, beaten

3 cups flour

2 cups water at room temperature (more if necessary)

1 tsp. salt

Filling:

2 lbs. frozen spinach (boil for one minute, cool, and squeeze well to remove excess water; see note)

1 cup whole milk ricotta cheese

1 egg

$1/4$ tsp. freshly grated nutmeg
(ground nutmeg in a jar is fine, too)

1 cup grated parmigiano cheese

1 lb. fresh mozzarella cheese,
cut in $1/2$-inch-square strips

1 tsp. salt

NOTE: *The best way to squeeze the excess water is to take a handful of cooled cooked spinach at a time and squeeze it between the palms of your hands.*

Béchamel:

$1/2$ cup flour

8 Tbsp. sweet butter (1 stick)

pinch of salt

milk (enough to make a liquidy batter)

PREPARATION

For the crepes:

• In a bowl, mix the eggs, salt, flour, and water a little at a time. Add more water if necessary in order to make a fairly liquid batter and to make sure that flour does not ball up.

• In an 8-inch crepe pan or an 8-inch greased frying pan over medium heat, add a ladle of the batter and quickly swirl it around the pan to cover it all around. Cook until light golden brown. Flip the crepe and brown the other side.

• Repeat step above making crepes until all batter is used. Set each crepe aside after cooking.

• Makes 15 to 20 8-inch crepes.

NOTE: *Make sure the crepes are quite thin. If you find they're too thick, add more water to the mixture and use less than a ladle of it.*

For the filling:

• In a food processor, add the spinach, ricotta cheese, parmigiano cheese, egg, nutmeg, and salt. Process at low speed or pulse for 10 to 20 seconds. Set aside.

For the béchamel:

• In a small pan, melt the stick of butter, then add the flour and salt. Mix well and keep mixing with a wooden spoon until smooth. Cook at low heat until the mixture starts turning light golden brown. Start adding the milk slowly, mixing at the same time. As the béchamel gets thick, add more milk and keep on adding and mixing until you get a smooth, not-too-thick consistency (on the liquidy side is preferred).

• Make sure the mixture doesn't stick to the bottom of the pan.

For the cannelloni di crespelle:

• Put the crepes on a flat surface and fill each one with some of the spinach filling, making sure that all the crepes have about the same amount of mixture on them. Then put 1 or 2 slices of the mozzarella on each one; roll them up and set one next to the other, in a single row in a greased baking pan.

• When the pan is full all around, pour the béchamel sauce over the rolled crepes and bake in a preheated oven at 350° F. for 20 to 30 minutes.

• Serve hot. Great as a main course, sprinkled with parmigiano cheese.

• Serves 6 to 8.

Ravioli Ignudi

(Naked Ravioli)

This dish is one of my Top Ten Favorite Meals. In fact, it recently won my mother first place in a cooking contest in Italy. The panel of judges deemed it "exceptional." And no wonder—it's delicate, tasty, and very unusual. Way to go, Mamma! Her prize was a $2,000 living room set. Not bad for a 90-year-old woman.

INGREDIENTS

2 lbs. fresh spinach (or frozen)

1/2 lb. ricotta cheese

2 cups grated romano or parmigiano cheese

2 eggs, beaten

$\frac{1}{2}$ tsp. freshly grated nutmeg (ground nutmeg from a jar can be used)

1 cup flour

1/2 lb. sweet butter

**10-15 fresh sage leaves
(fresh sage is a must)**

salt and pepper to taste

PREPARATION

- In a large pot, bring water and 1 Tbsp. of salt to a boil. Put in the fresh, washed spinach (or frozen spinach) and simmer for 10 minutes. Drain the spinach in a colander and set aside to cool.

- Take clumps of the spinach and use the palms of your hands to form balls about 3 inches in diameter. Squeeze as much water as possible out of them and set aside.

- Take each ball and with a sharp knife cut it into about 1/4-inch slices (this helps to cut up the stems of the spinach). When all the spinach balls are cut up, place in a large bowl. Add the romano or parmigiano cheese, the ricotta cheese, the eggs, the nutmeg, salt and pepper. Mix everything well; the slices will become part of the mixture. Set aside in the refrigerator for an hour to firm up.

- With a tablespoon pick up some of the mixture and again with the help of your hands start rolling the mixture between your palms, forming naked ravioli the size of your thumb in an oval shape. As you work, set them in a dish with some flour on the bottom to prevent them from sticking. Continue until all of the mixture is finished.

- Roll all of the ravioli in the remaining flour on a plate. Set aside in the refrigerator.

- Place the butter and sage in a small pot and melt the butter over medium heat until it starts getting foamy and a little darker. Remove from heat and set aside.

- Fill a large pot with water and bring to a boil. When the water is boiling gently, add the ravioli and cook for about 2 to 3 minutes. They will start floating. Take them out and gently set them on preheated plates. Pour the hot butter and sage over them. Sprinkle with some grated cheese and serve hot (this is a must).

- Can be a main dish or a side dish.

- Serves 4.

TRIAL AND ERROR

You'll make mistakes as you learn gourmet cooking. Don't worry about it—that's the only way to learn.

Cipolle Gelatinate

(Onions in Gelatin)

This dish is time-consuming but presents so beautifully that you'll be inordinately proud! It tastes pretty good, too.

INGREDIENTS

6 large white onions

1/4 lb. mortadella

1 cup pitted black olives

2 Tbsp. canned whole corn (drain well)

1 egg

2 Tbsp. finely chopped parsley

1/4 lb. lean ground beef

1 clove garlic, minced

1/2 package unflavored gelatin

4 Tbsp. butter (1/2 stick)

1 cup grated parmigiano cheese

1/2 quart water reserved from cooking onions

salt and pepper to taste

PREPARATION

- Peel off the first layer of skin from the onions and discard. Boil the onions in 1 gallon of water for 30 to 45 minutes. Retain the water.

- With a spoon, gently dig out the center of each onion until you reach the other end. Discard the dug-out center. Set aside the centerless onions.

- Put the ground beef, mortadella, pitted olives, chopped parsley, garlic, drained corn, parmigiano cheese, salt and pepper, and the egg in a food processor. Process for 1 minute or until mixed well.

- Fill every onion with an equal amount of mixture. Top each off with a small piece of butter and cap with a round piece of aluminum foil.

- Arrange the onions standing up, one next to the other, in a greased pan. Bake in a preheated 350° F. oven for 25 minutes.

- Remove from oven and cool.

- Cut them into $1/2$-inch medallions and arrange in layers in a Jello-type mold or bundt pan. Filter the reserved cooled water through a piece of cheesecloth. Mix with the $1/2$ package of gelatin, following the instructions on the package. Pour this over the onion medallions in the mold. Refrigerate. After it sets, put a plate on top of the mold and turn it over quickly. (To ensure that the *cipolle gelatinate* slides out easily, first loosen it by briefly lowering the mold into a big pot of hot water—but only for a second!)

- Serve this gelatinous dish cold. Makes a great side dish for meat, poultry, or fish.

- Serves 4 to 6.

THE TUSCAN LOAF

In Tuscany, our bread has a hard crust and no salt. If it has salt in it, it's not Tuscan bread.

Foglie di Salvia Ripiene

(Giant Sage Leaves Stuffed)

My mother would make 30 or 40 of these when she was expecting guests. She used to say, "You cannot say no to this appetizer, so I want to make sure I have more than enough." You can find fresh sage leaves in a good produce store. If they don't have the giant ones, you can use two ordinary-sized ones. I like to put them on a platter as an appetizer when I have a party. I serve it hot, though it's still good when it cools down. Buon appetito!

INGREDIENTS

12 large sage leaves

12 mozzarella strips, about **1** inch long and $\frac{1}{2}$ inch wide

2 slices rosemary-flavored cooked ham (I prefer Boars Head), cut into strips the long way, **1** inch wide, to make **12** strips

4 Tbsp. flour

salt to taste

water

4 cups oil for frying

1 small can anchovy fillets (optional)

PREPARATION

- Wash the largest leaves you can find; set flat on a large dish. Put a small piece of ham on each leaf (enough to cover each leaf); then put the mozzarella strips on top of each leaf horizontally. You can include an anchovy now, if you wish. Gently roll each leaf until it's a tight tube and then skewer with a toothpick to seal.

- When all of them are rolled and ready, make a loose batter with the flour, the water, and salt. The batter should be loose but not dripping off the rolled-up leaves when you are dipping them in. In a frying pan, heat the oil to a medium heat (drip a drop of the batter into the hot oil; if the oil splatters a little, it's hot enough).

- Dip the rolled-up leaves into the batter and one by one set them gently into the hot oil, making sure they don't stick together. Let them fry on one side until golden brown. Turn them and finish frying them until golden brown.

- Serve hot as an appetizer.

- Serves 6.

Spaghetti al Tartufo

(Spaghetti with Truffle Sauce)

Truffle is a type of fungus that grows underground. It comes in two varieties: white and the more pungent black. The rarest—and therefore the most sought after and expensive— is the white truffle, which mainly comes from the town of Alba, in the region of Piedmont in Italy. They have a white truffle festival every year. The black is also very tasty. Both are expensive. You can find them in a good Italian gourmet store or by typing "truffles" into a search engine on the Internet so that you can order them online. They're sold canned, frozen, and in jars—and sometimes can be shipped to you fresh when they're in season. In Umbria, the villagers used pigs and dogs to sniff for truffles. Young Mafalda would take her best pig and go to the hills. She had to make sure no one followed her—competition was fierce!

INGREDIENTS

1/4 of a truffle, shaved

1 lb. spaghetti

4 Tbsp. sweet butter (1/2 stick)

1 cup heavy cream

salt and freshly ground pepper
(freshly ground pepper is a must)

2 cups grated parmigiano cheese

PREPARATION

- In a frying pan, melt the butter and add the grated truffle. Sauté for 5 minutes at low to medium heat. Add the heavy cream and bring to a boil. Set aside.

- Meanwhile, cook the spaghetti the way you like it (al dente or well done); strain, and while still hot add the butter, heavy cream, and truffles, plus 1 cup of the parmigiano cheese. Stir well.

- Serve hot. On each serving, sprinkle some freshly ground pepper and the rest of the parmigiano cheese.

- Serves 4.

SALAD

Italians don't have a wide variety of salads. Give us tomatoes, lettuce, and oil and vinegar— and we're happy.

CHAPTER EIGHT

Mafalda and Renato: Partners in eating...

My parents were very much in love—with each other and with food. My mother loved to cook, and my father loved to eat. If we were out somewhere and he couldn't sit down to eat his lunch at exactly noon, he got cranky. As soon as we got home, he'd say, "Do we ever eat in this house?" And he would pace until the food appeared.

Once when my parents were visiting us here in New York, we stopped at McDonald's for lunch. Mafalda is an adventurous eater (she doesn't think much of people who won't try new foods), and she loved her Big Mac.

My father grudgingly ordered french fries and ate them. He couldn't believe that this fast-food stop was being passed off as "lunch." He stayed in a bad mood until Anna reassured him that there would be a good meal on the table at dinnertime.

My mother cooked for Renato every day of their marriage until his death in 1995. She knew how important it was for him to have his meals on time, and preferably at home. She still says to me, in Italian, "Your father, he liked to have his feet dangling under the table."

She could whip up something for him (and us kids) even when there wasn't much money. *Coccoli (Fried Dough Balls)* was something she could pull together without having to spend any money at the store. And she could do it at the drop of a hat, when Renato came home unexpectedly and announced, "I'm hungry." She could wave her magic wand and *Spaghetti Aglio e Olio (Spaghetti with Garlic and Oil)* was on the table in minutes. When she'd had a very busy day and knew she couldn't fuss for that night's dinner, she would buy fennel bulbs, and *Pinzimonio (Fennel with Olive Oil)* would make a speedy appearance, or she'd produce an equally timely *Stracciatella (Egg Drop Soup Italian Style)*. And she never had to be coaxed into making my father's favorite Saturday afternoon lunch—the simple *Tonno e Fagioli (Tuna and Cannellini Beans)*.

Though he liked having Mafalda cook for him, my mother's food obsession could sometimes be too much even for Renato. She'd always talk about what to prepare for the next meal while we were still eating the one in front of us. I remember one time when my father, his belly close to exploding after one of her power lunches on a Sunday afternoon, looked across the table at his wife and said, "What? You're going to talk about food now?"

Even so, Mafalda and Renato were well suited to each other when it came to eating. On one of their visits, their flight wasn't due until late at night, and after picking them up at the airport we didn't get home until one in the morning—at which point we promptly sat down to a hearty meal, including a bottle of wine. The next morning, Anna wasn't going to prepare a breakfast for them, assuming they'd be too full. I said, "Anna, make the breakfast. It won't bother either one of them. They could digest a brick."

She didn't know them like I did!

Coccoli

(Fried Dough Balls)

This is a typical Florentine dish. It dates back to medieval times when food was a luxury for most people, and what they had on hand at the time had to count. This unfortunate state of affairs was repeated again during two devastating world wars. We became very fond of this dish, which is now on the menu at fancy restaurants in Florence.

INGREDIENTS

4 cups flour

1 ¼ oz. active dry yeast

1 tsp. sugar

1 ½ cups milk

stracchino cheese (fresh,
soft brie can be used instead)

salt

oil for frying (should be 1 to 2 inches deep in
the frying pan for the coccoli to float freely)

PREPARATION

- Warm the milk, but don't let it get hot. In small bowl, dissolve the yeast in the milk. Add the sugar and 1 cup of the flour, and mix well with a wooden spoon. (A wooden spoon is a must; metal utensils prevent the rising process of the yeast.)

- Set aside covered in a warm place; check after 10 or 15 minutes—if the mixture is bubbling, that means it's ready.

- Put the remaining flour and the yeast mixture in a large bowl; slowly add the rest of the milk, mixing at the same time. Make sure it's neither too heavy nor too liquid. (When you pick some up with a wooden spoon, it should not come off easily; you should have to push it off with your finger.)

- In a deep frying pan, heat the oil to a medium frying temperature. When the oil is hot, use a wooden spoon to scoop up a spoonful of the mixture, and with your finger push it gently into the oil. Repeat as many times as the size of your frying pan allows (no more then 10 is advisable). Do not turn. The *coccoli* will turn by themselves when the down side is ready. (They really do turn, as long as they have enough room in the pan—so don't crowd them.) Fry until a light golden color.

- Remove them from the oil and drain on paper towels. Sprinkle with salt. For each serving, while very hot, put sliced cheese over the coccoli so it will melt on them.

- Serve very hot. You can place the coccoli in the oven for a few minutes at 300° F. to keep them hot.

- Makes a great appetizer or side dish.

- Serves 4.

Spaghetti Aglio e Olio
(Spaghetti with Garlic and Oil)

See if you, too, like Mafalda, can whip this up in a few minutes.

INGREDIENTS

1 lb. thin spaghetti, cooked according to your preference (al dente or well done) and kept hot

2 cloves garlic or more if you wish, crushed with the flat of a knife

3-4 Tbsp. extra virgin olive oil, heated in a small pan and kept hot

1 cup grated parmigiano cheese (romano cheese is okay, too)

1 small piece of dried hot chili pepper, crushed into flakes

PREPARATION

- Crush the two garlic cloves on a cutting board. Meanwhile, heat up 4 dishes in the microwave or regular oven, or in a pot with boiling water. When the dishes are hot, one by one rub them vigorously on the inside with the crushed garlic. Then add the previously cooked spaghetti that was kept hot, the oil, the flaked hot chili pepper, and a handful of parmigiano cheese. Stir well and serve immediately (the hotter the better). The rest of the cheese can be sprinkled on top after serving.

- Serves 4.

HERBS

These herbs are more pungent dried than fresh—rosemary, sage, fennel seed, bay leaf, oregano, and dill.

Pinzimonio

(Fennel with Olive Oil)

Here is a dish that's extremely simple, very healthy, and delicious. You can find fresh fennel bulbs (a.k.a. anise) in the produce section.

INGREDIENTS

1 fennel bulb, cut into eighths (quartered and then each of the four pieces cut again in half)

½ cup extra virgin olive oil

1 tsp. coarse kosher salt

1 tsp. freshly ground pepper

PREPARATION

- Put the oil in a cup. Add to it the salt and pepper and stir well. Let it sit for 5 minutes. Pour the oil into two cups. Each person should dunk a fennel piece into their own oil mixture, making sure to stir while dunking. Bite a piece off and enjoy.

- Serves 2.

Stracciatella

(Egg Drop Soup
Italian Style)

My mother would whip this up for my father in no time, and I remember she did the same for me. I would come home from school, starving as usual, and this dish would appear out of nowhere. "Hi, Mama," I would shout upstairs to her. "I'm hungry. Do you have anything ready?" She'd appear at the top of the landing and say, "I just made some stracciatella. Eat it before it gets cold." I swear my mother had a sixth sense when it came to food.

INGREDIENTS

(Remember this rule: With this dish, it's always 1 egg for each person.)

4 eggs, lightly beaten

1 quart chicken, beef, or even vegetable stock

1 cup grated parmigiano or romano cheese

1/4 tsp. grated lemon zest

1 or 2 pinches of nutmeg (nutmeg can be overpowering, so go easy with it)

1 Tbsp. heavy cream or half-and-half

salt and pepper to taste

PREPARATION

- In a bowl, add the eggs, cheese, lemon zest, nutmeg, and cream. Mix well. Set aside.

- Bring the stock to a boil, lower the heat, and add all of the ingredients. Bring to a boil again, and cook stirring constantly for 3 minutes. Add salt and pepper to your taste.

- Serve hot with cheese sprinkled on top.

- Serves 4.

THE NOSE KNOWS

If you're out for a romantic evening, make sure your date eats the same amount of garlic you do.

Tonno e Fagioli

(Tuna and Cannellini Beans)

A very simple dish, prepared with very simple ingredients, but it was my father's favorite. When he could have this for lunch, he was a happy man. And I agree with him wholeheartedly.

INGREDIENTS

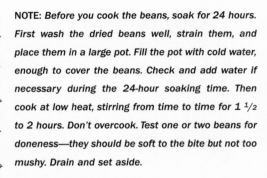

½ lb. dried cannellini beans or dried white kidney beans (soaked in water for 24 hours and then cooked; see note at right), or 1 16-oz. can cannellini beans or kidney beans

1 large red onion, thinly sliced

1 can solid white tuna in water (canned tuna must be used for its taste and texture)

4 Tbsp. extra virgin olive oil

3 or 4 fresh sage leaves, rolled between your fingers to bring out the flavor

salt and pepper to taste

ON COOKING SMELLS

To keep your house free of cooking odors, cook in someone else's house.

NOTE: *Before you cook the beans, soak for 24 hours. First wash the dried beans well, strain them, and place them in a large pot. Fill the pot with cold water, enough to cover the beans. Check and add water if necessary during the 24-hour soaking time. Then cook at low heat, stirring from time to time for 1 ½ to 2 hours. Don't overcook. Test one or two beans for doneness—they should be soft to the bite but not too mushy. Drain and set aside.*

PREPARATION

- Squeeze the water from the can of tuna. Put the tuna in a medium bowl and crush it coarsely with your fingers or a wooden spoon. Add the sliced onion and mix well. Add the cannellini beans, oil, salt and pepper.

- Mix again gently, keeping the beans whole. Add the sage last. Mix again.

- Refrigerate for about an hour for the flavors to blend.

- Mix again before serving.

- Serve cold. Eat this with a crusty loaf of Italian bread and maybe a glass of red wine.

- Serves 2 to 4.

Botticelli tried, but the real Three Graces in
Florence are Basil, Rosemary, and Sage...

CHAPTER NINE

When Mafalda comes to visit...

There's never a dull moment when my mother comes to stay with us. She has remained a vivacious woman all through the years, interested in everything around her. But of course what stands out most in my mind are her never-ending escapades involving food.

Minnows at the meadows

Many years ago, when my parents came to the U.S. regularly for visits, my family and I would often take them on weekends to Sunken Meadow

Park on the Long Island Sound to picnic with relatives.

One Sunday, two of my cousins noticed that Mafalda was spending all day wading around in the shallows. The two women, sitting on beach chairs and fanning themselves, chuckled and agreed that "at least poor Mafalda is keeping herself busy on this hot summer's day."

They were pretty sure she was trying to do what the men were doing with nets out on the boat—catch minnows—and they felt bad because she didn't seem to be catching any.

No one was more surprised than they when Mafalda appeared in front of them at the end of the day with a big grin on her face. From the top of her one-piece bathing suit, my mother pulled out one minnow after another. You could have plopped minnows right into my cousins' mouths they were open so wide!

When she wasn't catching her own minnows by hand, Mafalda's attention would be riveted by what the men might be bringing back in their net. My wife Anna tells me (I would be out on the boat) that when Mafalda would spot us bringing the catch in, she would shake Anna and say, "*Vieni, vieni.*" ("*Come, come.*") All my wife wanted to do was sit on her blanket and draw pictures (she's an artist), but she felt compelled to get up for the sake of her excited mother-in-law. I guess you could say my mother's zest for life has always had that kind of infectious quality. It's always been right there on the surface for everyone to see—and share.

No rest for the food weary

At 10 o'clock one night, during one of her visits, Mafalda found extra porgies in the freezer. She decided to cook them, right then and there, for our cat Midnight.

Cries of protest rang out from family members in the bedrooms upstairs, where for the next few hours the smell of cooked fish wafted up.

Mafalda couldn't understand why anyone would be annoyed. On the one hand you had perfectly good porgies not doing anybody any good in the freezer. And on the other you had a perfectly good cat (well, sometimes) who would enjoy a treat. What she did was only natural, wasn't it?

Did Grandma hide the food again?

My mother has always made a lot of food during her visits, but often she hides it, much to the bewilderment of my family. I think this is a food-conserving habit she acquired during World War II when food and other supplies were scarce.

At my house we see her baking, for instance, but we can't always find what she baked. She once baked **Cenci**, a fried dough pastry, and it filled our kitchen with tantalizing sweet smells for hours.

When my two sons went hunting for the *cenci* later that night, they couldn't find it. The next day, Anna opened a kitchen drawer—and there it was, hiding in the back.

Buy a bouillon cube? Why?

My mother makes her own beef bouillon. Never mind that it takes more hours than there are in a day. She says her bouillon is real and healthful, and so she named it **Sincero**.

When she makes her bouillon at our house, she takes over the kitchen for a very, very long time. In fact, she takes over the kitchen for a very, very long time even when she's not making homemade bouillon.

Actually, Anna's a good sport about her mother-in-law taking over in the kitchen. She likes learning from Mafalda, especially when it comes to the uses of herbs and other natural remedies. When Mafalda was 15 years old and living in Umbria, she went to work at her aunt's apothecary, where they made medicine by hand. Mafalda has passed on to Anna her knowledge of which plants provide relief for which ailments.

There's only one thing about Mafalda's visits that Anna objects to. Mafalda has what Anna calls the World War II mentality, prevalent among those who survived the hardships in Europe in the 1940s. That way of looking at the world doesn't allow for washing machines to be used as often as we're used to in more prosperous times. Rather than indulge in the "luxury" of the washing machine, Mafalda leaves dirty, wet dishtowels to dry all over the kitchen.

Once Anna plunked six or seven of them off the kitchen counters and appliances and made it known they were "going into the washing machine."

Alas, Mafalda doesn't visit as often anymore. She's 90 years old now, and though still frisky, she has to be careful.

We miss her regular visits.

Mafalda, the gastronomic herald

One thing you can say about my mother: She's no snob. She loves Italy and its own special foods, but she also appreciates what the United States has to offer gastronomically.

She would often collect flyers at our supermarket that were advertising sales on steaks, lamb, pork chops, and other meat items, just so she could show her friends that "Americans do eat good food."

When she would pack to go back home, she'd stuff her suitcases with such American items as cans of tuna ("they make it better here"), boxes of aluminum foil ("there's more foil in them"), and My-T-Fine Lemon Pie Filling and Jello No-Bake Cheesecake ("we never heard of these in Italy!").

Exploding jars

When I was a child, one night my family and I were sitting at the dinner table when we heard explosions, one after the other, coming from the pantry.

When I saw the stricken look on my mother's face, I knew the worst had happened.

My mother had spent days grinding tomatoes, cooking marinara sauce, and then canning. She had inadvertently canned during a full moon when, as everyone in Italy knows, it will not be successful.

Mafalda was stoic as we began the cleanup. But we knew how hard she had worked and how bad she felt.

Years later, when Mafalda came to visit us, she was the victim of another explosion. She had packed jars of home-

canned porcini mushrooms into her suitcase—a special treat for me. Her suitcase was stored in the baggage compartment of the plane and apparently underwent severe changes in air pressure. When she arrived at the house and opened her suitcase, porcini mushrooms were splattered over everything.

Anyone else would have given up. "Too many explosions," they would have said. "I'm done." Not my mother. She cans to this day. It would take an explosion of gigantic proportions to get her to stop.

What she made for us

Besides making anything we asked for, Mafalda would usually cook a few staples that I really enjoyed having in the house. One was **Pummarola (Puréed Tomato Sauce)**, which you can freeze in small containers and use anytime. And another was **Salsa Piccante (Pungent Sauce)**, which you can store in the refrigerator for long periods of time. You can use it on just about any dish.

And we've always marveled at how she uses up any leftovers in our refrigerator. **Pizza Margherita (Pizza with Artichokes, Mushrooms and Ham)**, which I knew from my childhood, is one of those "use what's available" dishes. **Riso Millegusti (Thousand-Flavor Rice)** is a more recent concoction of hers and demonstrates her deft touch at combining ingredients. It's one of her many talents that I hope I've inherited.

Cenci

(Fried Pastry Dough)

This is a common pastry in Italy. "Cenci" means "rags." The name comes from the fact that, like a rag, the dough can take any shape. Let your imagination run wild. My mother makes the dough into works of art—a bow tie, a ribbon, a knot, a rose.

INGREDIENTS

4 cups flour

2 tsp. anise extract (if not available, use 2 tsp. anise seeds, crushed very, very fine to make a powder)

6 Tbsp. sweet butter at room temperature

1/3 cup sugar

2 eggs, beaten

pinch of salt

1 tsp. grated lemon zest

1 envelope pure vanilla powder (if not available, use 1 tsp. pure vanilla extract)

some rum or Vinsanto, enough to make a breadlike dough

some oil for frying

PREPARATION

- Put the flour in a bowl and add all the ingredients except the rum or Vinsanto and the frying oil. Mix well, then slowly add rum or Vinsanto until it forms a bread-like dough. Keep working for 5 to 10 minutes until smooth. Divide into 2 to 4 parts to make it easy to roll. On a flat surface, use a rolling pin to flatten the dough. The thinner you make it, the better it is. Once the dough is very thin, take a pizza cutter and start to cut the dough in irregular shapes of about 3 inches by 4 inches. Remember, let your imagination run wild.

- In a deep frying pan, heat enough oil at medium heat to ensure that the *cenci* can float without touching the bottom. Fry a few of the *cenci* at a time. Make sure they don't burn—they cook rather fast. They should look pale golden brown.

- Set them aside to cool, then sprinkle with powdered (confectioners) sugar and serve.

- Great for dessert with coffee or whenever you feel like having a treat.

Sincero

(Homemade Beef Bouillon)

Look at the amount of salt used! Because of it, Sincero lasts (in the refrigerator) practically forever. It's a nice staple to have around—use it whenever you would use a bouillon cube.

INGREDIENTS

2 lbs. very lean ground beef (the leanest you can get)

4 large carrots, chopped

several stalks celery hearts, the strings removed and chopped (enough to equal the carrots)

1 large white onion, chopped

1 cup chopped basil

1 cup chopped parsley

2 cups salt

PREPARATION

- In a pressure cooker containing 1 quart of water, add all of the ingredients except the salt. Cook for 20 to 25 minutes under pressure. If you don't have a pressure cooker, use a conventional pot, increase the water to 4 quarts, and cook covered for 1 ½ to 2 hours.

- Let cool. Add 4 cups cold water. With a blender at purée speed, purée a little at a time until very, very smooth. Feel it between your thumb and index finger for super smoothness. When smooth, add the salt and mix well. Place back in the pot and cook at low to medium heat to evaporate, about 2 to 3 hours. Stir from time to time to prevent the purée from sticking to the bottom.

- The mixture will look like a heavy paste. Let it cool. Put in jars and refrigerate. Use for soups, or add to roasts, gravy, sauces, and stews.

- Use sparingly; do not add salt when using because of the high salt content. Taste for proper seasoning.

Pummarola

(Puréed Tomato Sauce)

You'll need a blender to make this because everything gets puréed. It's so easy to keep containers of this frozen and take them out whenever you want to make some spaghetti. You put a little parmigiano cheese on top— and you've got yourself a meal and a half, without much work. I've got some pummarola in the freezer right now.

INGREDIENTS

1 16-oz. can whole tomatoes

8 Tbsp. butter (1 stick)

1 large onion, chopped

2 cloves garlic, minced

1 carrot, chopped

1 cup chopped fresh Italian parsley

1 cup chopped fresh basil

1 celery stalk, chopped

salt and pepper to taste

PREPARATION

- In a deep pan, melt the butter. Add the onion, carrot, parsley, and celery. Sauté until translucent. Then add the garlic, salt and pepper, and sauté another 5 minutes. Add the tomatoes and cook for 20 to 25 minutes. Let cool for about 1 hour.

- When cooled, put all of the above in a blender. Blend at high speed for about 1 minute or until all of the ingredients are completely puréed.

- Serve very hot.

- Serves 4 to 6.

Salsa Piccante

(Pungent Sauce)

You can use this as a condiment on just about anything. Serve it in a bowl, and let everyone take some to use as they wish. You can refrigerate it for months as long as you keep a layer of olive oil on top to seal in freshness.

INGREDIENTS

½ cup finely chopped fresh parsley

2 cloves garlic, finely chopped

½ cup bread (no crust)

1 hard-boiled egg, finely chopped

1 tsp. relish

1 tsp. mustard

2 Tbsp. olive oil

½ cup red wine vinegar

freshly ground pepper to taste

pinch of hot pepper (optional)

1 anchovy, finely chopped (optional)

PREPARATION

- Soak the bread in the vinegar, then squeeze well.

- Put all of the ingredients in a food processor or blender (if either one is not available, mix by hand), and process for one minute. Taste to see if there is enough salt and pepper (now is the time to add any if necessary).

- This pungent sauce is great for garnishing fried dishes, broiled or grilled meats, roast poultry, and grilled fish.

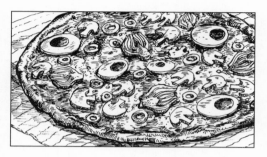

Pizza Margherita

(Pizza with Artichokes, Mushrooms and Ham)

When I was growing up, leftovers were never thrown out—they were reincarnated as a new dish. Whenever we had a diverse selection of leftovers, my mother would make this pizza, and it always tasted great!

INGREDIENTS

4 cups flour

3 hard-boiled eggs, thinly sliced

10-15 Spanish olives (with the red pimiento in the center), thinly sliced

1 cup sliced mushrooms

1 cup canned artichoke hearts in oil (drained), thinly sliced

1 lb. tomatoes, canned or fresh (drained of excess water)

1 tsp. oregano

3 or 4 slices ham (any kind), cut into small pieces

1 tsp. sugar

1 packet active dry yeast

1/2 lb. mozzarella cheese, shredded

1 cup milk

1/4 cup olive oil

salt and pepper to taste

1/4 cup water at room temperature

PREPARATION

- Put the yeast in a small bowl; add the water and stir well. Add the sugar and 2 Tbsp. flour. Mix well with a wooden spoon (avoid metal when making yeast mixtures). Cover and set to rise in a warm spot for approximately 5 minutes. You will notice bubbles forming in the bowl.

- Cook the tomatoes for 10 minutes with 1 tsp. sugar, 2 Tbsp. olive oil, and salt. Last, add the oregano. Set this aside.

- In a bread machine (you can also use a food processor, or just make the dough the old-fashioned way—by hand), mix the remaining flour, the yeast base, a pinch of salt, and the cup of milk together. Knead it (by machine or by hand) until smooth to the touch (add more milk if too heavy or more flour if too soft).

- Divide into 2 loaves. Place each in a greased bowl and cover with a clean kitchen towel. Set aside to rise in a warm, dark place.

- If you make a cross with a knife on top of each loaf, you'll notice the incisions starting to open up as the loaves rise. The loaves will almost double in volume in about 1 to 1 1/2 hours. The pizza dough is now ready to use.

- Start rolling the dough with a rolling pin and the palms of your hands, making it quite thin. Put it into 2 round or square ungreased baking pans. Brush the top of the dough with olive oil. Spread the tomatoes on top. Let it rise again for approximately 1/2 hour.

- Then put in a preheated 500° F. oven for a short time (not too much cooking). When they are half cooked (the crust should be golden brown), spread the mushrooms, ham, olives, artichokes, sliced eggs, and mozzarella cheese on top. Add salt and pepper on top of the mozzarella. Cook until the mozzarella melts.

- Serve hot.

- Serves 4 to 6.

Riso Millegusti

(Thousand-Flavor Rice)

All these flavors taste terrific together.

INGREDIENTS

1 cup uncooked arborio rice

2 slices salami (totaling $1/4$ lb.), cut into small cubes

$1/4$ lb. prosciutto, cut into small cubes

2 hot dogs, cut into small cubes

$1/4$ lb. Swiss cheese, shredded

$1/4$ lb. peas

$1/4$ lb. cooked small shrimp, cut into small pieces

$1/4$ cup pitted green olives, cut into small pieces

$1/2$ cup pitted black olives, cut into small pieces

2 Tbsp. capers

3 medium pickles, cut into small pieces

1 cup mushrooms sliced

1 or 2 slices roasted yellow or red pepper, cut into small pieces

juice of 1 lemon

$1/2$ cup olive oil

salt and freshly ground pepper

PREPARATION

- Put the rice in a cooking pan. Add water to cover the rice by about 1 inch. Bring to a boil, lower the heat, and cover. Cook covered until all of the water is evaporated, approximately 10–15 minutes.

- Transfer the cooked rice to a large bowl; let it cool. Then add all of the ingredients one at a time. Mix well for 2 minutes. Refrigerate.

- Serve cold.

- Serves 4 to 6.

HEAVENLY BREAD

Fresh bread is a religion in Italy.

While Dante was waiting to get a glimpse of Beatrice, he was also hoping to get a piece of her crostata . . .

CHAPTER TEN

Proud to be Florentine...

Florentines have many reasons to be proud. Their city is considered the intellectual heart of Italy. It's the birthplace of the Italian language and Italian literature, and a world-renowned center of art, overflowing with famous statues, paintings, and architectural masterpieces.

In Florence we're also very proud of our gastronomical heritage. One dish in particular has a story attached to it that everyone in Florence can recite. That dish is **Arista (Roast Pork Loin),** and it's a staple of our cuisine.

The name derives from an ecumenical council that was held in Florence in 1430 to attempt to settle the differences between the Greek and Roman churches. The Florentines wanted to prepare a very good and very typical Florentine meal for the council attendees. So they served roast pork loin seasoned with rosemary, salt, and pepper.

As they ate, the Greeks began to exclaim, *"Arista, arista!"* ("Good, good!") And the name has stuck to this very day. You can go into any supermarket or delicatessen in Tuscany and ask for *arista*. You'll get the same dish that the Greeks enjoyed so much.

I make my *arista* (mostly for guests because it gives you plenty to serve them) in an Italian brick oven (called a *fornetto*) that I built in my backyard. (You can go on the Internet to find prefab kits for this type of oven). The advantage is that you'll get a nice crust on the outside of the pork if you use such a wood-burning oven.

Arista is typically served at weddings with roasted potatoes and another dish called **Fagioli all' Uccelletto (Beans Cooked Like Small Birds).**

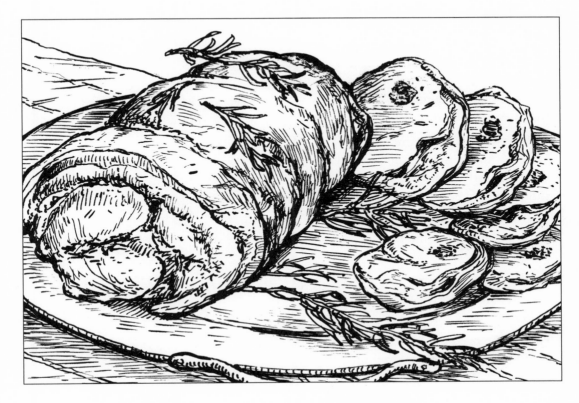

Arista

(Roast
Pork Loin)

My mother used to recite an old poem when cooking pork roast. It went like this, "Mai troppo cucinar l'arrosto di maial che nemmeno il gatto lo vorra` mangiar!" ("Never overcook the pork roast. If you do, not even the cat will eat it!")

INGREDIENTS

4 lbs. pork loin with bone

2 Tbsp. fresh rosemary leaves

1 cup dry white wine

10 whole cloves

4 fresh rosemary sprigs (for garnish)

4 cloves garlic

1/4 cup extra virgin olive oil

salt and freshly ground pepper

some peeled potatoes for roasting
(large potatoes should be quartered)

PREPARATION

- Finely chop the rosemary and garlic together. Using a sharp knife, make several cuts near the bone of the pork loin and stuff the combined garlic and rosemary into the slits.

- Make some shallow slits in different places on the outside of the pork loin. Combine the salt, pepper, and oil, and rub this mixture generously all over the meat. This will give it a crisp skin.

- Stick the cloves into the pork in several places.

- Pour the wine into a roasting pan and place the meat in the pan, resting on its bones.

- Preheat the oven to 350° F. and roast for 1 ½ to 2 hours. Baste from time to time. Do not turn!!

- About 1 hour into the cooking time, add the potatoes to the roasting pan. Don't turn the potatoes until they're golden brown on top. Before that, they will unstick on their own if you shake the pan around. After they turn golden brown, turn them over and baste them.

- I suggest using a meat thermometer so that you don't undercook or, worse, overcook the pork. When the internal temperature reaches 170° F., take the pork out of the oven and set aside to cool (this dish is better cold). Finish

roasting the potatoes in the pan juices until golden brown all around. Believe me, it will be a feast for the eyes and for the stomach.

- Serve the pork roast cold and the potatoes hot.

- Serves 6 to 8.

Fagioli all'Uccelletto

(Beans Cooked Like Small Birds)

Little birds have absolutely nothing to do with this recipe! This is actually one of my favorite dishes. It's very satisfying, especially if you dunk Italian bread in it and accompany your repast with a glass of good red wine. The Italian sausages are different from the ones usually available in the U.S. If you get your sausages from the supermarket, buy the ones that come in a wheel shape with no fennel seed.

INGREDIENTS

1 lb. dried white kidney beans, or some other long white beans

1 16-oz. can whole tomatoes, coarsely chopped

¼ lb. Italian pancetta, coarsely cut (similar to bacon but without the smoky taste; any good Italian deli should have it, but you can substitute thick-sliced bacon)

3-4 cloves garlic, gently crushed with the flat part of a large knife

6-7 fresh sage leaves

½ cup olive oil

salt and freshly ground pepper

5-6 spicy Italian sausages, poked with a fork and browned all around

PREPARATION

• Soak the beans for at least 12 hours, drain, and return to the pot. Add cold water, just enough to cover the beans, and cook at medium heat for 30 to 40 minutes, making sure that the water level stays just above the beans. Drain the beans and set aside.

• In the same pot, add 4–5 Tbsp. of the olive oil, the garlic, sage, and pancetta. Sauté until the garlic is golden brown; add the beans and stir for 1 minute to allow the flavors to blend. Add the tomatoes, sausages, salt and pepper, and let cook covered at low to medium heat for about 15 to 20 minutes.

• Serve hot.

• Serves 4 to 6.

FOOD PRESENTATION

Decorate the food on the serving plate with the main herb of the recipe. For instance, the pork dish *arista* should be presented with sprigs of rosemary as a garnish.

*Della Robbia knew that these angels
would get hungry eventually . . .*

CHAPTER ELEVEN

To the "other" woman in my life...

It wouldn't be right if I didn't use at least one of my wife's recipes in this book. It wouldn't be politically correct, you might say.

Seriously, I want to acknowledge that without Anna's support and honest opinion about my cooking over the years, many of these recipes would not be as successful as they are.

I also want to thank her for the many hours she has spent illustrating this book, deftly illustrating my mother in different situations and accurately capturing the variety of dishes we've included. Her talent is (and always has been) awe-inspiring to me, and now it has become an integral part of this book I wrote to honor my mother.

Anna has played and is still playing a major role in my life. Without her and my parents, I wouldn't be the happy man I am today.

My mother said this to my wife when we got married 30 years ago: *"Anna, ricordati che gli uomini vanno presi per la gola!"*

A rough translation: "Remember, Anna, a man has to be caught through his stomach!"

Mafalda gave Anna a copy of an old (1800s) Italian cookbook titled *La Scienza in Cucina: L'Arte Di Mangiar Bene (Kitchen Science: The Art of Good Eating)*, by Pellegrino Artusi. Many of the recipes Anna and I have used through-out the years we've been raising our family in the United States came straight from this dog-eared old book.

One recipe that did not come from the venerable cookbook, and did not come from my mother, is one that Anna developed on her own. No slouch in the kitchen herself (her mother, Mira, from Croatia, is an excellent cook), Anna always gets compliments when she presents what I will call **Pollo Fritto all' Anna (Anna's Famous Fried Chicken).**

My mother, Mafalda, and my dearly departed father, Renato, loved the way Anna made fried chicken. My father was never crazy about chicken, unless it came from a farmer and not the supermarket. But it was different when my wife cooked it.

Every time my parents came to visit from Italy, my

father would ask my wife to make the chicken "the way you make it." That was the greatest compliment possible. He would then rave about it at the dinner table, saying risky things like *"Allora, Mafalda, come mai il pollo non lo fai mai cosi` come fa` l` Anna?"* ("Why, Mafalda, do you never make the chicken the way Anna makes it?")

I would be looking down, shaking my head in disbelief for what my father had just said and anticipating a sharp reply from my mother. I figured she'd say something like, *"Si perche`a casa nostra cosa io cucino spazzatura?"* ("By the way you're talking, back home I'm cooking garbage?")

But the retort never came. And that's because—and yes, this is true—Mafalda herself loved Anna's chicken.

Pollo Fritto all' Anna

(Anna's Famous Fried Chicken)

INGREDIENTS

**1 whole chicken cut up, or 2 lbs.
chicken breast cutlets**

2 eggs, beaten

1 ¹/₂ cups breadcrumbs

¹/₂ cup flour

vegetable oil for frying

salt

PREPARATION

- Trim excess skin off the chicken
  pieces, wash and pat dry. Dip the
  pieces in the flour first, then in the
  eggs, and last in the breadcrumbs.
  Make sure all sides are well coated
  with the breadcrumbs. Set aside.

- Fill a deep frying pan about halfway
  full with the frying oil. Set the heat
  to medium high, and when the oil
  is very hot but not boiling, start
  putting a few pieces in, but be sure
  not to crowd them.